THE LONDON COMPLAINT

A Celebration of the Capital's Maladies

also by GEOFF NICHOLSON

The City Under the Skin
Walking in Ruins
The Lost Art of Walking
Gravity's Volkswagen
Sex Collectors
The Hollywood Dodo
Bedlam Burning
Female Ruins
Flesh Guitar
Bleeding London
Footsucker
Everything and More
Still Life with Volkswagens
The Errol Flynn Novel
Day Trips to the Desert
The Food Chain
Hunters and Gatherers
Big Noises
What We Did on Our Holidays
The Knot Garden
Street Sleeper

GEOFF
NICHOLSON

THE LONDON COMPLAINT

A CELEBRATION OF THE CAPITAL'S MALADIES

HARBOUR

First published as a paperback original by
Harbour in 2016
Harbour Books (East) Ltd, PO Box 10594
Chelmsford, Essex CM1 9PB
info@harbourbooks.co.uk

A CIP record for this book is available
from the British Library

ISBN 978 1 90512 830 3

Typeset by Antony Gray
Printed and bound in the UK by
TJ International, Padstow, Cornwall

Contents

There's a hole in the world like a great black pit
and the vermin of the world inhabit it
and its morals aren't worth what a pig could spit
and it goes by the name of London.

Stephen Sondheim, *Sweeney Todd*

ONE

Exquisite Zest: An Introduction

Of making books about London there is no end. The result may not necessarily be wearying to the flesh, but it can certainly be overwhelming to the reader and book buyer. The texts multiply, sometimes aiming for a grand overarching project, sometimes dividing London into ever smaller, ever more obsessive and particular segments. The sections in the bookshops expand, the shelves sag, the memory cards in e-book readers fill up. Elsewhere the reading lists and bibliographies lengthen. Nobody can read it all, it's hard enough even to keep track.

Diversity and a unique selling point are the name of the game. Each volume attempts to stake out its own London territory: geographically, historically, conceptually. The traditional, the romantic, the eccentric, the secret, the criminal, the literary, the political, the fetishistic, all crave attention, jostling spine to spine, cover to cover, sometimes competing, sometimes complementing, sometimes contradicting one another.

Sometimes there's name-brand recognition, so that certain books offer us the London of Dickens or Sherlock Holmes or Jack the Ripper, the Beatles or Virginia Woolf or Harry Potter. Of course there are many off-brand names too, versions of the city created by authors too obscure or eccentric or unreadable to merit our current attention.

But for all their variety, novelty and diversity, what all these texts have in common is that, in however perverse a way, each of them is a kind of love letter to the city, a display of affection, evidence of a crush. The degrees of passion vary, and the love takes a great many forms, some unrequited, some unreciprocated, but I don't believe I have ever met anybody who loved London completely, simply, absolutely, without any reservations or criticism. You might argue that's the way it always is with love: it's never a source of unbroken, unalloyed bliss. We're not blind to the loved one's faults, we simply decide to accept and live with them. We lovers know these faults better than anyone, and we remain in love not in spite of the faults, but because of them.

Nevertheless, and this could be a manifestation of love too, a great many people – residents, visitors, tourists, commuters, politicians, novelists – complain about London. They complain long and hard. They *enjoy* complaining about London. The complaining is a kind of safety valve, a form of therapy, a talking cure. People feel better for venting, for airing their grievances, and for knowing that others share their complaints and see the imperfections in the love object. If you need something to bitch and moan about, London gives you so much material, so many opportunities. But I think it's more than this. I'd suggest this is a condition, perhaps psychological, perhaps medical, perhaps neurological, something chronic and recurring, though not one found in the textbooks – the London Complaint.

It would, no doubt, be possible to compile a dour, humourless, accusatory book that was just a list of grievances, a catalogue of all the many things that people think are wrong with London. I believe that would be a very dull read, and this definitely isn't that book. But sometimes this bitching and moaning about London achieves a kind of critical mass; the condition manifests itself in interesting ways, with a wit, a stature, a profundity that becomes a crucial part of our experience of the city, and that's what this small book acknowledges. What you have here is an ambivalent celebration of our feelings and complaints about London, a book that also celebrates our ambivalence and our ongoing condition.

*

The complaints, the symptoms if you like, are many and various, though most them are very familiar. We all know, or think we know, what ails London. The place is expensive, dirty, potentially dangerous, ridden with crime and vice. The air is bad. There are too many people, certainly too many tourists. Public transport is slow, crowded, inefficient. Driving's impossible. The city goes to bed too early. Who would argue otherwise?

And yet certain complaints seem to contradict each other, which is not to say that they necessarily cancel each other out. London is supposedly dull and grey and boring, yet there's no peace and quiet to be had there. It's overcrowded yet everybody's alone. People are unfriendly and inhibited yet there are moments when the entire city turns into a giant bacchanal.

There are too many super-rich people, but too many beggars as well. The place is too insular for some, too cosmopolitan for others. It's stuck in the past yet it's awash in vacuous trendiness. It thinks very highly of itself, but nothing's ever as great as it's cracked up to be. There are security cameras everywhere and yet you never feel safe. And so on.

You want a quick sampling of some famous complaints and complainers from history? Of course you do.

In the *Chronicle of Richard of Devizes of the Time of King Richard I*, written in Latin, *circa* 1192, as a satirical 'travel guide', offering advice to young French Christians thinking of visiting England, the narrator writes, 'Si nolueris habitare cum turpidis, non habitatis Londonie.' (If you do not want to live among wicked people, do not live in London.)

Six and a half centuries later, Flora Tristan would have had no argument with that. 'In London all classes are deeply corrupted. Vice comes to them early,' she wrote in her *London Journal* in 1840. And a century after her, Noël Coward has a character say, in a sketch titled 'Law and Order', 'I don't know what London's coming to – the higher the buildings the lower the morals.'

There has long been the argument that it was the city itself that was the corrupting influence on people: something in the air or the environment or the housing conditions, something caused by having too many people crammed together in too small a space. 'In London it is always a sickly season,' says Mr Wodehouse in Jane Austen's *Emma* (1816). In *Brief Lives,* written piecemeal towards the end of the seventeenth century, John Aubrey says of the Earl of Rochester, 'his youthly spirit and opulent fortune did sometimes make him doe extravagant actions. He was wont to say that when he came to Brentford the devil entered into him and never left him till he came into the country again to Adderbury and Woodstock.'

And certainly there's the sense that London is a place separate and different from – and worse than – the rest of the country. Benjamin Disraeli in *Tancred* tells us that 'London is a modern Babylon' – this was in 1847. For William Cobbett, in *Rural Rides* (1822–6), London was the 'great wen' on the face of the nation. Sir Arthur Conan Doyle has Dr Watson say, in the opening of *A Study in Scarlet,* 'I naturally gravitated to London, that great cesspool into which all the loungers and idlers of the Empire are irresistibly drained,' though it was the corrupt and complex nature of the city that presented Sherlock Holmes with most of his best cases, and Conan Doyle with his best stories. Am I the only one who thinks Holmes is essentially a Londoner who goes off the boil when he gets to the Reichenbach Falls or the Grimpen Mire? There's a certain relief when we learn that the hound of the Baskervilles was in fact bought 'from Ross and Mangles, the dealers in Fulham Road'.

The Czech writer Karel Čapek visited London in 1925 and wrote about the experience in *Letters from England.* 'Of course I went to look at Baker Street, but I came back terribly disappointed. There is not the slightest trace of

Sherlock Holmes there,' which to a writer of fiction really shouldn't have come as much of a surprise. Today there's not much trace of Oliver Twist or Mrs Dalloway or Johnny Fortune to be found in London either, but there are now numerous signs of Holmes – a museum, a hotel, a statue and a choice of walking tours led by guides in deerstalkers.

Still, disappointment is often a large part of the London experience, the reality of which may not measure up to the visitor's expectations. 'I first came to London when I was twenty-two and working as a roadie. Having watched the *News at Ten* all my life, I thought Big Ben was going to be massive, but I was underwhelmed.' The malcontent speaking there is Noel Gallagher of Oasis.

V. S. Naipaul, not in general a fellow traveller with Noel Gallagher, seems to have experienced something oddly similar. In his novel *Half a Life,* published in 2002 but describing life in the 1950s, the protagonist, Willie Somerset Chandran, an Indian immigrant, is disappointed by just about everything in London.

> He knew that London was a great city. His idea of a great city was of a fairyland of splendour and dazzle, and when he got to London and began walking about its streets he felt let down . . . The only two places he knew about were Buckingham Palace and Speakers' Corner. He was disappointed by Buckingham Palace. He thought the maharaja's palace in his own state was far grander, more like a palace, and this made him feel, in a small part of his heart, that the kings and queens of England were impostors, and the country a little bit of a sham.

And here's Steve Coogan's creation, Alan Partridge, trying to sell his autobiography on the station concourse in Norwich, and yelling at the travellers getting on the London train, 'Off to London, no doubt. Go to London! I guarantee you'll either be mugged or not appreciated. Catch the train to London, stopping at Rejection, Disappointment, Backstabbing Central and Shattered Dreams Parkway.'

Partridge's writers, though not Partridge himself, understand that the other side of disappointment may be a nagging sense of self-doubt, the feeling that you haven't lived up to what London demands of you. None of that for Noel Gallagher or V. S. Naipaul, obviously.

And no doubt there's some disappointment in the reaction of Lorelei Lee, the heroine of Anita Loos's wonderful *Gentleman Prefer Blondes* (1925). She has a chapter titled 'London is Really Nothing' and tells you why she thinks that. 'For instants they make a great fuss over a tower that really is not even as tall as the Hickox Building in Little Rock, Arkansas.'

But she was wrong with that chapter title, surely. You may not like London, it may not treat you well, it may chew you up and spit you out, but whatever else you may say, however you slice it, whether you like it or not, however much you complain about it, London really is *something.*

*

We should probably consider Dr Johnson, since so many other people do. He's famously, repeatedly, often uncritically quoted as saying, 'When a man is tired of London, he is tired of life.' This is generally taken to be a piece of positive, upbeat boosterism for the city, but as always, context is everything.

The words are reported by James Boswell in his *Life of Johnson,* in an account of a conversation that took place between the two of them on 20 September 1777. Boswell lived in Scotland at the time and was only an occasional visitor to London, and this is Johnson's response to Boswell's wondering whether, 'if I were to reside in London, the exquisite zest with which I relished it in occasional visits might go off'. Johnson's reply, rarely quoted in full, reads: 'Why, Sir, you find no man, at all intellectual, who is willing to leave London. No, Sir, when a man is tired of London, he is tired of life; for there is in London all that life can afford.'

Well, this is not a straightforward reply, since Boswell, clearly, was perfectly willing to leave London all the time, in order to go back to Scotland. So perhaps there's a deliberate insult in there. Is Johnson saying that since Boswell is constantly willing to leave London he isn't 'at all intellectual'? He wouldn't be the last to make that observation. The reply certainly has nothing to say about

Boswell's potential loss of 'exquisite zest'. And insult or not, the reply does raise the question of just how many people in London, in Johnson's time or any other, are intellectual in any sense whatsoever, and whether they could care less.

Johnson had certainly felt less positive about London as a younger man. In 1738, when he was a little under thirty, he published 'London: A Poem in Imitation of the Third Satire of Juvenal'. In Juvenal's original, the character Umbricius is tired of the vices of ancient Rome and goes to live in Cumae, twelve miles west of Naples. In Johnson's poem a character named Thales leaves London for Wales, and Johnson writes of London:

> Here Malice, Rapine, Accident, conspire,
> And now a Rabble Rages, now a Fire;
> Their Ambush here relentless Ruffians lay,
> And here the fell Attorney prowls for Prey;
> Here falling Houses thunder on your Head,
> And here a female Atheist talks you dead . . .
>
> Prepare for Death, if here at Night you roam,
> And sign your Will before you sup from Home.
> Some fiery Fop, with new Commission vain,
> Who sleeps on Brambles till he kills his Man;
> Some frolick Drunkard, reeling from a Feast,
> Provokes a Broil, and stabs you for a Jest.

And yes indeed, as the poem clearly says, London, like any city, will contain plenty that isn't even remotely intellectual, and for some people this may well be the attraction. Many might think that malice, fire, ambush and the occasional falling building is a small price to pay for the more personal and urgent pleasures of the flesh. The young James Boswell was very much in this category.

In 1762, aged twenty-two, he arrived in London and kept a diary of what he got up to. The results were lost until 1950 when the rediscovered manuscript was published as *Boswell's London Journal.* Johnson was evidently aware of the diary and had advised Boswell to destroy it. It's not hard to see why. Boswell doesn't come out of it especially well, positively revelling in the seamier side of London. The journal is a cheerful account of drinking, whoring, cockfighting, gambling, watching the occasional public execution and getting involved in the odd brawl. It's a young man's book, boastful, self-centred, sometimes self-lacerating, occasionally very moralistic, but not unlikable, and not unobservant.

After a drunken dispute with his landlord, Boswell goes to see the local magistrate. He writes,

> I went to Sir John Fielding's, that great seat of Westminster justice. A more curious scene I never beheld: it brought fresh into my mind the ideas of London roguery and wickedness which I conceived in my younger days by reading *The Lives of the Convicts*, and other such books. There were whores and chairmen and greasy blackguards of all denominations assembled together.

Yes, Boswell is disapproving, but it reads as though he's also enjoying a certain *nostalgie de la boue* at observing and being part of this grotesque scene.

Nevertheless, after nine months or so in London, Boswell did leave, not because he was appalled by the vice and crime, or because he was tired of life, but because (like any number of promising young men before him) he simply hadn't got on as well in London as he'd expected to. Despite being well connected and quite the brown nose, he hadn't received the success and advancement he thought he deserved. On 5 August 1763 he left London for 'foreign parts'.

I haven't been able to track down a book titled exactly *The Lives of the Convicts*, though a great deal of what we'd now call true-crime literature was published and read in eighteenth-century Britain, much of it emanating from London, where the population was generally more literate than in the rest of the country. One book that might stand as an example of the genre is a three-volume work, published in 1735, titled *Lives of the Most Remarkable Criminals who have been condemn'd and Executed for Murder, Highway Robberies, House-Breaking, Street-Robberies, Coining, or other Offences; From the Year 1720, to the Present time . . . Collected from Original Papers and Authentick Memoirs*. It's thoroughly London-centric.

The author writes,

> Although the Insolency of those Street-Robbers . . . be at present too recent a Fact to be questioned; yet possibly in future Times 'twill be thought an Exaggeration of Truth to say that even at Noonday, and in the most open Places in London, Persons were stopped and robbed, the Offenders for many Months

> escaping with Impunity; untill these Crimes became so frequent, and the Terrors of Passengers so great, that the Government interposed in an extraordinary Manner; a Royal Proclamation issuing out, offering one Hundred pounds Reward for apprehending any Offender, and also promising Pardon to any who submitted and discovered their Accomplices.

The authorities relied on grasses even then.

*

Dr Johnson was perfectly well aware of the downside of living in London, and in his famous quotation he actually puts his finger on the problem: Any city that has 'all that life can afford' is inevitably going to contain a lot of things that a lot of people don't want. The fact that certain other people actually *do* want these things only adds to the difficulties. London is a place of wildly competing interests and desires that are only ever partially compatible.

And we can end this introduction with the views of world traveller and honorary-Londoner Paul Theroux, who first visited the city in 1965, 'I remember travelling through Clapham Junction looking at the backs of the houses and thinking, "How can people possibly live in this place?" ' Later however, he moved into one of those houses, and was perfectly happy living there and raising a family. And having got to know the place he said, famously, 'The man who is tired of London is tired of looking for a parking place.'

TWO

Some Bigger Pictures

The first recorded mention of London – as Londinium – was by Tacitus in Book 14 of his *Annals*, written about 109 AD. Plenty of others must have known about the place and discussed it long before then, but they didn't write down their thoughts. In consequence, that work by Tacitus also contains the first record of Londoners complaining. Tacitus is himself a little dismissive of London, describing it as 'undistinguished by the name of a colony', but the complaining done by Londoners, in fact the 'tears and weeping' as he describes it, doesn't seem at all unreasonable.

In 60 or 61 AD Gaius Suetonius Paulinus, the Roman Governor of Britain, knew that an attack on the city was coming from the east, in the form of Boudicca's forces of Icenae, Trinovantes and others. He had to decide whether London was worth defending. Despite the efforts of the not-entirely-disinterested locals to persuade him to stay and fight, he decided it was not. He knew he was outnumbered and so he and his troops abandoned the city and retreated to fight another day.

According to Tacitus, the civilian inhabitants of Londinium were invited by Suetonius Paulinus to go with him, and only those who were 'chained to the spot by the weakness of their sex, or the infirmity of age, or the attractions of the place, remained behind'. The attractions must surely have been strictly limited at that point, and since Tacitus is such a supporter of Suetonius Paulinus, it's just conceivable that the offer of evacuation wasn't quite as generous and all-inclusive as the *Annals* suggests.

Anyway, Suetonius Paulinus and his men, and presumably at least some London civilians, left, Boudicca arrived, burned the city and slaughtered everyone remaining in it. This occurred within Tacitus' lifetime, though he was about five years old at the time, but clearly he wasn't an eyewitness.

A more detailed account was written about a hundred years later by Cassius Dio, by which time Boudicca had been thoroughly demonised. Dio tells us that her armies hung up the 'noblest and most distinguished' of the women of Londinium, cut off their breasts and sewed them to their mouths, so that it looked as if they were eating them. We can only speculate, but I'd think that sewing a severed breast to a human mouth would have been a difficult and time-consuming business, and a hard one to pull off in the circumstances. The invaders were also, perhaps more plausibly, said to have impaled the women, lengthwise, on skewers.

This may be misogyny or indeed misogynistic fantasy, and at this remove it's impossible to distinguish between fact and exaggerated, self-serving fiction. Of course these histories were written by the victors. But undoubtedly tens of thousands of inhabitants of first-century

Londinium were slaughtered one way or another by Boudicca and her forces.

*

The first person to write an extended, detailed account of London was John Stow (1525–1605). In 1598 he published *A Survay of London, Containing the Originall, Antiquity, Increase, Moderne Estate, and description of that city*. Then in 1603 he published a revised and expanded second edition, and he was still working and rewriting up to the time of his death, two years later.

Stow was a tailor by trade but by calling he was a historian, antiquary and collector of books and manuscripts (some of them considered deeply seditious at the time). He was also a great walker, describing London as though he was walking across the city, an urban explorer, a psychogeographer a good few centuries before, and perhaps the begetter of, a whole tribe of writers, historians, documentarians, street photographers and even TV presenters who have used walking as a method for investigating London. He has a lot to answer for.

Like anyone who tries to deal with London as a whole, and looks at it squarely, Stow had plenty of criticisms and complaints. And since he wasn't just describing the London of his day, but the entire history of the city as he knew it, some of his concerns now seem to us more pressing than others.

He could, for instance, still summon up plenty of righteous indignation against Edward I, who had invited himself to the store house at the Temple, saying he wanted to take a look at the crown jewels, which were there for safe keeping. But once inside, surrounded by the strong, thick, secure walls of the place, the king rummaged through other people's coffers and made off with a thousand pounds. The fact that this happened in 1283, three hundred years before Stow was writing, doesn't make him any more forgiving.

Sometimes Stow's complaints look a lot like nostalgia for the London he used to know. He frets about the growth of the city, he frets about the disappearing fields around the city. He writes, for instance:

> In the East ende of Forestreete is More lane: then next is Grubstreete, of late yeares inhabited for the most part by Bowyers, Fletchers, Bowstring makers, and such like, now little occupied, Archerie giving place to a number of bowling Allies, and Dicing houses, which in all places are increased, and too much frequented.

That's right, you know the neighbourhood's going to the dogs when the archers move out and the bowling alley moves in.

And sometimes, for example when he discusses the problems of wild pigs roaming the city, it seems he could be describing another planet, not just a different time. The modern reader accepts that roaming pigs might not have been entirely easy to live with, but even so, it sounds like a certain amount of fun. Not to Stow and the citizens of London however. The pigs caused 'such a nuisance that at an early date men were appointed to kill all that were found loose in the streets'.

Expanded editions of Stow's survey continued to be published after his death, often containing maps and illustrations. Some of the editing and updating was wayward, but there was a 'perfected', or at least unlikely-to-be-improved-upon, edition by John Strype, often referred to as 'Strype's Stow', published in 1720, and at that point titled *A Survey of the Cities of London and Westminster.* It was several times longer than Stow's original, incorporating all kinds of new material, much of it necessitated by changes, growth and events in London – plague, fire, a regicide, a Commonwealth, a Restoration, a huge population boom – that had created a city wildly different from the one Stow knew. Even so,

much in the new edition was dictated by Strype's own personal tastes and idiosyncrasies.

John Strype (1643–1737) was a clergyman, historian and biographer. He wrote a four-volume history of the Reformation, and his biographical subjects included Thomas Cranmer. He was a moralist and a true believer, and he seems to have regarded London as a battlefield for the war between vice and virtue. He took for granted that the city was a place crammed with sin and lewdness, but he took great delight in the many forms of punishment available in London at that time, methods that could be used to chastise and 'correct' sinners. Book 5, Chapter 3 is titled, 'The late Endeavours used in the City for the restraining of Vice'.

These were many and various. Reading Strype it's easy to believe that there were stocks, pillories, cages and whipping posts on every street corner. Bridewell for instance, once a palace for Edward VI, was now 'A Place for the Correction of such idle and loose Livers, as are taken up within this Liberty of Westminster, and thither sent by the Justices of the Peace for Correction; which is whipping, and beating of Hemp, (a Punishment very well suited to Idleness)'. Clearly, the whipping of 'loose livers' would be even more of a full-time occupation today than it was then.

But there were many others who needed punishing in Strype's London: dishonest millers and bakers, pickpockets, harlots, bawds (male as well as female), scolds, women who ate or served meat during Lent. Also butchers. Strype tells us:

> In the . . . Year 1560, One rid about London, with his Face toward the Horse Tail, for bringing in and selling meazle Bacon at Market. [I *think* this means that the pig had measles.]The same Man the next Day was set on the Pillory, and two great Pieces of his meazle Bacon over his Head, and a Writing set up, shewing his Crimes: And that about two Years before, he was punished for the same Offence.

John Strype's edition of the *Survey* adheres to Stow's notion of exploring the city as though on a walking tour, and he adds a few 'perambulations' or circuit walks of his own. It's very hard to see that word 'perambulation' without thinking of Nikolaus Pevsner and his guides to London, and eventually most of Britain, in his *Buildings of England* series, later titled *The Architectural Guides*.

Pevsner perambulated all over London, and he knew perfectly well that he was working in a tradition: he mentions Stow and Strype in the London volumes. Like Stow's, his work has been re-edited and revised by subsequent, diverse hands, though his editors have been a good deal more sympathetic than Stow's.

*

Nikolaus Pevsner (1902–83) was born in Leipzig into a Russian-Jewish family, and visited England as a child with his parents, but his first visit to London as an adult came in 1930 when he was doing research for a course of lectures he was about to deliver at the University of Göttingen. He based himself in a hotel in Bloomsbury and evidently found London overwhelming, describing in his letters home 'the noise of the traffic which rages all over town, without interruption, and the smell of petrol, and the constant need to be careful when crossing the road'.

He wasn't very enthusiastic about some of the architecture either. He wanted Modernism and it was in short supply.

> From Regent Street and Kingsway I have now seen something of the monumental architecture of today. I think it's mostly dreadful. In Berlin everything is modern and almost always good and satisfying – in London I haven't seen a single building that we would regard as giving a modern effect.

Even so, at this time he did contemplate writing a book to be called *The Making of London,* and subsequently conceived the idea of a large multi-volume work, not just on London but on the whole of England. Circumstances seriously delayed both those projects. Being Jewish, he was denied his academic post in 1930s Germany, and moved to England to teach at the University of Birmingham. However, when the war started he was put in an internment camp in Huyton, outside Liverpool, actually a council estate. Fortunately, he had friends in high places and was released; he spent the rest of the war in London, and there found an ally in Allen Lane of Penguin who signed him up as an author.

The current version of Pevsner's *London* runs to six volumes, but the book had begun as just two: one volume, published in 1952, for the whole of London except Westminster and the City, and a second, published in 1957, for Westminster and the City. This caused some amusing consternation among the staff at Penguin. Editor Alan Glover (who had, it was said, once worked as a tattooed man in a circus) complained, 'I can only say that if I were walking from Charing Cross to the Bank making a rapid study of architecture I should be a bit disturbed at having to carry one fat volume in my right-hand trouser pocket and another fat volume in my left, and as you may have observed I am not over-particular about the set of my trousers.'

Pevsner was able to call on a number of sources to help with his own overview. There was the *Survey of London*, established in 1894 by C. R. Ashbee, though carried out by volunteers. And there was the *Royal Commission on Historical Monuments*, started in 1908 to make an inventory of all British buildings, earthworks and stone constructions up to 1714. By 1943 they'd extended this to 1850, making the task that much harder. Pevsner acknowledged these sources, but perhaps the entire project owed more to his long-suffering wife Lola, who travelled with him on many of his perambulations.

Although he did his research in advance, once on site he simply walked and looked. 'Nothing is supposed to be included which is not visible,' he wrote in that 1952 volume. But things were much complicated by the effects of the Blitz. He was walking through a ruined post-war city, even if he tried to make the best of it.

> Architectural losses are irreparable, but those who have seen the hideous shells of the Wren churches . . . and Chelsea Old Church, the brutal rents in the mellow red fabric of Gray's Inn . . . will one day, I feel sure, look up to what will be left with more respect and more love than their parents and grandparents.

Well, only up to a point. By the early sixties he was a full-blooded conservationist railing against planners and developers. In an interview with the *Listener* in 1962 he said,

> Sometimes I feel like emigrating, away from the country which viciously demolished Robert Adam's Adelphi, the finest piece of London's river front, and viciously destroyed Sir John Soane's interior of the Bank of England . . . I feel it again now that the Euston Propylaea are being viciously demolished . . .

Pevsner is generally seen as patrician, lofty, detached, austere, cold, not for him the wild poetic excesses of say Ian Nairn, though the two of them did work together briefly on Pevsner's guide to the buildings of Surrey. But detached or not there's plenty of personality in Pevsner's writing, and although he's not much of a complainer, when he does condemn or criticise a building the effect is all the more startling. So Dolphin Square is 'a huge lump', Piccadilly Circus is 'big, prosperous and unenterprising'. The Art Deco Hoover factory on Western Avenue is 'perhaps the most offensive of the modernistic atrocities along this road of typical bypass factories'.

The fact is, anybody who explores the streets of London and creates a catalogue of what is and isn't a significant building, is creating his or her own singular version of London. Pevsner creates a city in his own image and also a self-portrait. His books reveal the man even as they reveal the city.

*

Ian Nairn (1930–83) was not just revelatory in his writings about London, but positively exhibitionistic. Especially in his later television programmes, he displayed a doomed melancholy, a complaint not just against planners and architects but about the human condition.

His book *Nairn's London*, first published in 1966, followed in 1988 by a posthumous update, is much less wide-ranging than Pevsner. In the first line of the Preface he says, 'this guide is simply my personal list of the best things in London'. It has 450 entries. He finds a large number of pubs worthy of attention.

Nairn's unique selling point is his enthusiasm for London and its architecture, but he's also a great complainer. Hampstead, he tells us, 'is a bit of joke, though many of its inhabitants are deadly serious about it'. Highgate is an 'anthology of horror'; 12 Langford Place is 'sheer horror: a Francis Bacon shriek . . . it looks like a normal St John's Wood villa pickled in embalming fluid'; Waltham Cross is 'cruelly sited and cruelly restored'.

He also has complaints about London as a whole:

If there is a generalised sense of the capital – bright

> lights, red buses, swirling traffic – it is almost entirely due to the genius of John Nash, who in Regent Street gave the West End a trunk around which it could grow. Nash came from Lambeth, and he was every inch a cockney . . . But [now] everywhere the cockneys are pushed out and the cockney streets are pulled down – often with the best of sociological intentions . . . The human essence of the city is now in places that are nothing to look at: Brentford, Mitcham, Charlton, Tottenham, Plaistow, West Ham, Wembley. The old contract which bound clubman, chorus-girl and coster-monger together to form a city has been torn up, and London has moved into a limbo.

Nobody ever accused Nairn of underwriting.

*

So, if all surveys and overviews are ultimately personal, they must also be partial. Nobody knows or 'gets' the whole of London, because nobody ever could. Nobody could keep that much information in their head. Nobody could stay current. Google Street View attempts to give the perspective of a godlike, indifferent, impartial, eye in the sky, or at least the view from a camera perched on top of a car. We're able to look unflinchingly, and unseen, at people's homes, and maybe their gardens, and see what kind of car they have parked outside, occasionally see in through a window, but it's never clear that we're ever seeing anything that really matters. Paul McCartney recently had his London house taken off Street View for security reasons, although you can find the address online in half a second.

His fears are surely justified. If our personal version of the city reveals our personality, it must also reveal our fears. Here are some warnings from the 1900 edition of Baedeker's *London and Its Environs*:

> We need hardly caution newcomers against the artifices of pickpockets and the wiles of impostors, two fraternities which are very numerous in London. It is even prudent to avoid speaking to strangers in the street. All information desired by the traveller may be obtained from one of the policemen, of whom about 15,550 (about 300 mounted) perambulate the streets of the Metropolis . . . Poor neighbourhoods should be avoided after nightfall.

*

Surveys of London continue to be done, some much grander than others. Some are solo activities, some group efforts, some personal, some corporate. Some are more disinterested than others, but inevitably they all have angles, vested interests.

In recent years the Royal Photographic Society ran a project called 'Bleeding London', based on my novel of the same name, in which a character walked down every street in London. The plan was for participants to take a photograph – a good photograph with some aesthetic value, not just the equivalent of a Google Street View – of every single street in the *London A–Z* – 43,000 or so, depending on how you define a street. It was a wonderfully, overwhelmingly ambitious project, with the results shown online and at City Hall, but like any project of its kind, it was a series of images frozen in time, the way things looked for a fraction of a second on a given day. London didn't necessarily look like that a second before and probably wouldn't look much like it a second later. That, of course, might be the whole point of a certain kind of survey.

Charles Ashbee's *Survey of London*, the one referenced by Pevsner, is still very much in business after considerably more than a hundred and twenty years, though in a modern form. In 2013, it was taken on by the Bartlett School of Architecture at UCL, and continues to produce detailed architectural and topographical studies of the built environment, which are increasingly about environment as much as architecture.

It has an online presence, but the printed book seems its definitive form, and it extends now to fifty volumes. And these are not books for the casual London stroller. The two volumes on Battersea, run to over a thousand pages and cost £135.

But perhaps the most specifically commercial and certainly corporate overview is the London Office Crane Survey, which has been run by Deloitte, the international financial-services company, for the last twenty years. The survey tracks every office scheme being built across central London, 'looking ahead at the potential delivery of space and its future impact on supply in the market . . . widely used as a barometer of developers' sentiment and future office supply'. 'Peak office' is expected to hit in 2018.

The information is entirely business-oriented, although future historians are obviously going to find it an important source of information. The layman, on the other hand, may find himself not so much uncomprehending as alienated by the terminology, with its talk of 'strengthening leasing activity' and the 'growing popularity of tech-belt locations'. This is not how most of us see, much less survey London, but this is only proof, if proof were needed, that there are an infinite number of ways of seeing London.

And how high-tech is this survey? According to *World Architecture News*, 'the Deloitte London Office Crane Survey was carried out between April 2015 and October 2015. A team of researchers walked every street in central London, including the City, the West End, Docklands and the Southbank, recording all office construction or refurbishment of 10,000 square feet plus.'

I'm still not sure whether John Stow would have approved or not. Pevsner, I think, would not. Nairn, I think, would have objected violently and gone to the nearest pub.

THREE

Some Accommodations

Living in London isn't easy. Some would say it *shouldn't* be easy. That's how the herd gets thinned: the runts and the weaklings are found wanting and they slope off to the provinces. But if you're one of those who hangs in there, then London toughens you up, puts you on your mettle, makes you a better version of yourself. You have to accommodate yourself to the city, because the city absolutely won't accommodate itself to you. But that's OK. In the end you come out tougher, sharper, stronger, forged in the fire. That's one theory anyway. But first you've got to find somewhere to live.

A great many us have had the experience of being in London, sleeping on somebody's couch or floor, while we desperately try to find somewhere to live. You walk the streets and see tens of thousands, maybe hundreds of thousands of people, and you ask yourself, 'Where do all these people *live*?' The population of London is currently about eight and a half million, and the number of 'rough sleepers' (or homeless) is estimated at about six and a half thousand, so the vast, vast majority of people must live *somewhere*. There are moments when this seems very hard to believe.

Money is always an issue but it's seldom the only issue. Of course London is expensive, and historically Londoners have always spent a higher proportion of their income on accommodation than people in the rest of the country. But it's still not that simple. Yes, there's *some* relationship between what you pay and what you get, but it's seldom a strictly direct one. You rarely think you're getting what you're paying for, and even if you pay more than you can afford you rarely get what you want. Maybe you tell yourself that being overcharged for crummy accommodation is the necessary price for living in one of the world's great cities. Again, this is only a theory.

The forms of shelter change over time: boarding and lodging houses invariably described as 'seedy' or 'shabby', give way to bedsitters which are generally 'cramped', and they may give way to 'hard to let' council flats (hard to let for good reasons), and there are always shared flats, invariably 'chaotic'. Times change but the horror stories remain much the same – malfunctioning plumbing and heating, mad landlords, nightmare neighbours – they become part of our personal London narratives, and in some cases they get turned into art.

The heroine of Lynne Reid Banks's *The L-Shaped Room*, published in 1960, is Jane Graham, a young, unmarried, pregnant Englishwoman who's been thrown out of the family home by her father. She ends up in a boarding house.

> I didn't even bother to take in the details – they were pretty sordid . . . My room was five flights up in one

> of those gone-to-seed houses in Fulham, all dark brown wallpaper inside and peeling paint outside. On every second landing was a chipped sink with one tap and an old ink-written notice which said 'Don't Leave Tap Driping' [*sic*]. The landing lights were the sort that go out before you can reach the next one. There were a couple of prostitutes in the basement . . .

Quite a lot of detail there from somebody who 'didn't even bother to take in the details'.

That light switch on a spring-loaded timer is so very familiar. I lived with those a long time ago, when I first came to London. And, of course, sordid though it might be, the boarding house in this novel is full of lovable misfits as well as prostitutes. One of them is a Jewish writer who publishes a book titled *The L-Shaped Room.* When Lynne Reid Banks's novel was turned into a movie a couple of years after publication, Jane Graham had become Jane Fosset, a Frenchwoman, played by Leslie Caron.

If there's been a great London bedsitter novel I haven't found it yet, though I'd be happy to. But the bedsit seems to thrive in other forms outside of the novel: an episode of Hancock; a memoir by Tracy Thorn – *Bedsit Disco Queen*; a cookbook – *Cooking in a Bedsitter* by Katharine Whitehorn, first published in 1963 and still in print. And there are also various pop songs, the best of them being Soft Cell's 'Bedsitter'. It owes a mighty debt to Al Stewart's 'Bedsitter Images' and David Bowie's 'London Boys', but it's ultimately great in its own right.

Marc Almond's lyrics tell of wild Saturday nights out –

'Dancing laughing, Drinking loving' – followed by the Sunday-morning comedown when our hero listens to the radio and thinks about writing a letter to his mum. Then he looks in the mirror at 'the battle scars of all the good times' and then, despite some self-hatred, he starts it all over again.

There's a video accompanying the song, which, to my eyes, varies between the laughable and the excruciating – much eye-rolling from Marc Almond, shots of wandering the streets of Soho, then Almond at 'home' in a single bed, possibly even a camp-bed, in a bedsitter that's tatty yet looks surprisingly roomy, though maybe that's because it's a film set.

Still, what's great about the song is the passionate, plaintive, yearning quality of Almond's voice as he sings: 'And now I'm all alone, / In bedsit land, / My only home.' It's pained and melancholy and knowing and self-dramatising: I think most bedsit dwellers have been there.

There is also a great play and movie *The Bed-Sitting Room*, written for the stage by John Antrobus and Spike Milligan, and put on screen by Richard Lester. It's set in a post-nuclear London. Every visible sign of the city has been destroyed although the underground still runs: people even live in the carriages. Only twenty people are known still to be alive in England, but there is among them the late Queen's former charwoman, and survivors sing, 'God save Mrs Ethel Shroake of 393a High Street, Leytonstone,' since she was next in line to the throne when the real royal family was obliterated.

There's currently a launderette at that address, named Launderette.

The play and film's overarching absurdist conceit is that Lord Fortnum of Alamein – played by a gorgeously dotty Ralph Richardson – thinks he's turning into a bedsitting room. This doesn't make him happy – he'd much rather be turning into a stately home. Well, wouldn't we all?

*

Occasionally writers describe, or invent, brand new forms of accommodation and exploitation, as is the case in *Box and Cox*. That's the title of the 1847 play by John Maddison Morton, billed as 'a romance of real life in one act', and in fact based on a French original.

Mrs Bouncer, a London landlady, lets out the same 'decently furnished' room to two different men, each unaware of the other's existence. Box is a printer on a daily newspaper, who works nights and only needs the room in the day; Cox works days as a hat-maker, so only needs the room at night when Box is out. 'It was a capital idea of mine – that it was!' Mrs Bouncer tells the audience in an aside.

Of course complications ensue. Cox thinks that Mrs Bouncer has been using his room during the day, and complains to her that his coal keeps disappearing and there is 'a steady increase of evaporation among my candles, wood, sugar and lucifer matches'. He also complains that his room smells of tobacco smoke.

Mrs B	Lor, Mr Cox! you surely don't suspect me?
Cox	I don't say I do, Mrs B; only I wish you distinctly to understand that I don't believe it's the cat.
Mrs B	Is there anything else you've got to grumble about, sir?
Cox	Grumble! Mrs Bouncer, do you possess such a thing as a dictionary?
Mrs B	No, sir.
Cox	Then I'll lend you one – and, if you turn to the letter G, you'll find 'Grumble, verb neuter – to complain without a cause'. Now that's not my case, Mrs B.

Like all Londoners he thinks his complaints are entirely justified and in this case he's surely right.

*

Contentment is rarely part of the deal when it comes to London accommodation. Even when Londoners have found somewhere more or less tolerable to live, they constantly have the urge to improve their lot, to move out and up.

Back in the day when Anita Brookner was in full creative flight and writing a novel a year, she would always say in interviews how much she hated her pokey little flat. Many of the characters in her novels were in a similar position. At least she didn't have to worry about a landlord.

The relationship between landlords and tenants is rarely a sunny and uncomplicated one. For instance, according to Wilhelm Liebknecht's *Karl Marx: Biographical Memoirs,* published in 1901, when Marx and his family first arrived in London in 1849 and lived in Camberwell, 'There he had some trouble in consequence of the landlord's declaration of insolvency, the creditors having the privilege to re-emburse themselves with the furniture of the occupants, according to English law.'

And sometimes the relationship can turn murderous. Both sides have reasons to be fearful. In March 2000, Charalambos Christodoulides, a 'quiet, simple man' according to evidence at the trial, was murdered on the orders of his landlord Thanos Papalexis. Christodoulides was the sitting tenant, and caretaker, of a warehouse in Kensal Rise that Papalexis had bought a matter of days earlier and wanted to sell, untenanted, for a quick profit. Christodoulides didn't want to leave, and Papalexis was in a hurry, but up to that point it was a familiar enough story; situations of that kind, with people being paid to move out of their rented accommodation, arise in London every day. In this case, however, the negotiating process consisted of the tenant being tied to a chair, tortured to death and tossed into an inspection pit inside the warehouse.

By contrast, in March 2010 in Sutton, Stuart Crawford murdered his 'landlord and friend', Michael Ryan, by hitting him over the head repeatedly with a bat or hammer, then he hid the body in a roll of carpet, and stashed it behind a bookcase. At the Old Bailey trial Crawford was described as being of 'no fixed address' which I suppose is how it goes after you've murdered your landlord.

At least Joe Meek, the music producer, the Svengali behind the Tornados, creator of the hit single 'Telstar' and enthusiastic 'cottager', squared the circle and had the decency to kill himself after he'd killed his landlady. This happened in February 1967 at the combined home and recording studio he rented above a luggage shop at 304 Holloway Road.

The only account we have of events comes from Meek's assistant, one Patrick Pink, who was on the premises at the time, though not an eyewitness to all that happened. According to Pink, a depressed and increasingly desperate Meek deliberately provoked an argument with his landlady, Violet Shenton. Voices were raised, Meek killed the landlady with a shotgun, reloaded and turned it on himself. The argument probably didn't need much provoking. Meek had been slow in paying his rent and there had been too much noise coming from the studio, so Mrs Shenton surely had grounds for complaint on both counts. She hardly sounds like a Rachman.

*

Peter (originally Perec) Rachman was the eponymous epitome of Rachmanism, a term that entered the English language as a synonym for the exploitation and intimidation of tenants by unscrupulous landlords. Frankly it's surprising that it took so long to put a name to what is surely an ancient practice.

Rachman was a Polish immigrant who during the Second World War had fought with the Second Polish Regiment in support of the Allies. He pitched up in post-war London, and by the early 1950s had set up the Express Letting Agency in Westbourne Grove. It was a time of housing shortages, a growing immigrant population, and loosely enforced housing regulations. Rachman operated at the rough end of the market, with a substantial portfolio of properties, chiefly centred around Powis Square. According to evidence presented to the West London Rent Tribunal in 1959, the properties ranged from 'scruffy' to 'unfit for human habitation'.

If Rachman was worried by this, he didn't show it. He was chauffeured around in a Rolls Royce, accompanied by glamorous 'girlfriends', conduct unlikely to endear him to his poorer tenants, you'd have thought. The girlfriends may well have been prostitutes. He certainly rented out flats to working girls, and was eventually prosecuted for brothel-keeping.

In order to maximise his profits, Rachman bought properties with sitting tenants then chased them out, immediately increasing the value of the property. He didn't go as far as Mr Papalexis, and he did apparently pay some people to leave, but he also used strong-arm tactics: rats and itching powder placed in the beds; tenants sometimes returning home to find all their possessions out in the street; all-night parties held in the flats next door. Once the sitting tenants, mostly white, had moved out, Rachman subdivided the flats and let them to newly arrived, desperate and sometimes naïve black tenants, although not all these new arrivals were as naïve as all that. Some of them were happy enough to take money from Rachman to harass and scare off the existing tenants.

In recent years there's been some attempt to reassess Rachman, to suggest that he wasn't quite as much of a Rachman as has been claimed, or if he was, he was no worse than most landlords of that place and era. At least he did let out properties to black people which many landlords simply wouldn't do. Indeed, it may well be that his detractors were motivated by anti-Semitism.

There is certainly a good argument that Rachman's reputation is less about his being a slum landlord, and far more about his tangential connection to the Profumo affair, which didn't break until 1963, a year after his death. He had owned a property where Christine Keeler and Mandy Rice-Davies stayed, and he'd had 'affairs' with both of them. Even if he'd been a generous and blameless landlord this would surely have been enough to get him on the front pages. A famous *Private Eye* cover from 26 July 1963 shows Mandy Rice-Davies with a speech bubble that says, 'Do you mind? If it wasn't for me, you couldn't have cared less about Rachman.' Hard to disagree with that.

1963 was the year the *People* newspaper denounced Rachman as the head of an 'empire based on vice and drugs, violence and blackmail, extortion and slum landlordism the like of which this country has never seen and let us hope will never see again'. The television programme *Panorama* then 'exposed' Rachman as a 'big-time twentieth-century racketeer'. The fact that Rachman wasn't around either to defend himself or to be prosecuted only gave free rein to his detractors.

A few days before that issue of *Private Eye* hit the streets, on 23 July, Harold Wilson made a speech in Parliament for the Labour Opposition, which ran in part:

> Try as they may to play this matter down, Ministers know that the people of this country have been gravely shocked by what they have read in the national press and by what they saw on *Panorama* last Monday about the methods of slum landlords in London.
>
> Sometimes one turns over a stone in a garden or field and sees the slimy creatures which live under its protection. This is what has happened in these past weeks. But the photophobic animal world has nothing to compare with the revolting creatures of London's underworld, living there, shunning the light, growing fat by battening on human misery.

Can you imagine any contemporary British politician using the word 'photophobic'?

*

One of Rachman's most effective henchmen was Michael de Freitas, who later styled himself Michael X, 'the most famous black criminal in London over the last hundred years', according to Sukhdev Sandhu. After Rachman died he found a way to exploit the counterculture, and racial anxieties, by befriending luminaries such as John Lennon and Yoko Ono, and setting up the Black House, a sort of black-power commune, at 95–101 Holloway Road, about half a mile from Joe Meek's old gaff.

Incredibly, in 1967, de Freitas was the first non-white person to be prosecuted under the Race Relations Act, a measure designed to protect the black and Asian population of Britain against bigotry, but one which cut both ways. De Freitas had advocated killing any white man seen 'laying hands on a black woman': he was sentenced to twelve months in jail.

De Freitas was born in Trinidad, first came to Britain while working as a seaman, decided to stay and arrived in London after stops in Cardiff and Birmingham. He moved around a little within London and as he described in his 1968 autobiography, *From Michael de Freitas to Michael X*, came upon some of London's worst housing. He writes:

> It was impossible to believe you were in twentieth-century England: terraced houses with shabby, crumbling stonework and the last traces of discoloured paint peeling from their doors, windows broken, garbage and dirt strewn all over the road, every second house deserted, with doors nailed up and rusty corrugated iron across the window spaces, a legion of filthy white children swarming everywhere and people lying drunk across the pavement.

That's quite literary, isn't it? It partakes of a long tradition among writers of denouncing London slums while making literary capital out of them, although Michael X's portrayal has nothing on Dickens's 1838 description of Jacob's Island, the 'notorious rookery' in *Oliver Twist*, where Bill Sikes eventually meets his end.

Dickens had been taken there as a kind of slum tourist by the Thames Police, and his 'fictional' description runs in part as follows:

> Crazy wooden galleries common to the backs of half a dozen houses, with holes from which to look upon the slime beneath; windows, broken and patched, with poles thrust out, on which to dry the linen that is never there; rooms so small, so filthy, so confined, that the air would seem too tainted even for the dirt and squalor which they shelter; wooden chambers thrusting them-

> selves out above the mud, and threatening to fall into it – as some have done; dirt-besmeared walls and decaying foundations; every repulsive lineament of poverty, every loathsome indication of filth, rot, and garbage . . .

Ten years later Henry Mayhew's, non-fiction, account in a letter to the *Morning Chronicle* seems if anything even more lurid:

> On entering the precincts of the pest island, the air has literally the smell of a graveyard, and a feeling of nausea and heaviness comes over anyone unaccustomed to imbibe such an atmosphere. It is not only the nose, but the stomach that tells how heavily the air is loaded with sulphuretted hydrogen; and as soon as you cross one of the crazy rotting bridges spanning the reeking ditch, you knew, as surely as if you had chemically tested it, by the black colour of what was once the white-lead paint upon the door-posts and window-sills, that the atmosphere is thickly charged with this deadly gas.

Can you imagine any contemporary writer using the word 'sulphuretted'? Apart from Will Self, obviously.

De Freitas's description benefits from first-person experience, a comparative rarity in these matters. There is, however, one famous example of slum dwellers describing their own condition. In 1849, forty men and fourteen women, living in St Giles, an area known as Cock and Pie Field, wrote to *The Times* – the letter was published on 3 July:

We print the following remonstrance just as it has reached us and trust the publication will assist the unfortunate remonstrants.

The Editur of the Times Paper

Sur: – May we beg and beseach your proteakshion and power. We are Sur, as it may be, livin in a Wilderniss, so far as the rest of London knows anything of us, as the rich and great people care about. We live in muck and filthe. We ain't got no privis, no dust pins, no drains, no watersplies, and no drain or suer in the hole place. The Suer Company, in Greek St, Soho Square, all great, rich and powerfool men, take no notice watsodever of our complaints. The Stenche of a Gully-hole is disgustin. We all of us suffur, and numbers are ill, and if the Colora comes Lord help us.

Some gentlemens comed yesterday, and we thought they was comisheners from the Suer Company, but they was complaining of the noosance and stenche our lanes and corts was to them in New Oxford Street. They was much surprised to see the sellar in No. 12 Carrier St, in our lane, where a child was dyin from fever, and would not believe that Sixty persons sleep in it every night. This here sellar you couldn't swing a cat in, and the rent is five shillings a week, but theare are great many sich here sellars. Sur, we hope you will let us have our cumplaints put into your hinfluenshall paper, and make these landlords of our houses and these comishoners (the friends we spose of the landlords) make our houses decent for Christians to live in.

Some Accommodations

Praye Sir com and see us, for we are livin like pigs, and it aint faire we shoulde be so ill treted.

We are your respeckfull servents in Church Lane, Carrier St And the other corts.

There follows a list of fifty-four signatories. As far as I can tell, nobody has ever questioned the authenticity of this letter, and certainly nobody has ever doubted the awfulness of the conditions it describes, and I'm not about to do so now. And yet I can't help feeling it might be a literary construct. The 'illiteracy' seems a little forced and 'stage cockney'. Wouldn't at least one of the fifty-four signatories know someone, most likely a clergyman or a schoolteacher, who could have taken the letter and ironed out some of the problems with spelling and grammar? Or could it be that they *had* found such a person, who'd written the letter for them, in a literary approximation of these people's voices and writing abilities, retaining the errors as a show of authenticity? For better or worse, it does feel a bit too Dickensian.

*

Strictly speaking, Dickens is not considered a writer of 'slum fiction' – a genre essentially restricted to literature written in the last two decades of the nineteenth century by the likes of Walter Besant, Arthur Morrison, George Gissing, and Somerset Maugham in his *Liza of Lambeth* phase. The point here, of course, was not simply to describe the slums, not even to complain about them, but rather to imagine a new, better, slumless world.

In Besant's 1882 novel, *All Sorts and Conditions of Men*, a pair of 'do-gooders', Angela and Harry, disguise themselves as members of the working class and go to live in the East End – slumming in actual slums, though the word 'slum' appears nowhere in the novel. The word squalid is frequently used, however.

Angela and Harry are frankly insufferable. They eventually decide to set up a kind of Arts Lab:

> Enter in, my friends; forget the squalid past; here are great halls and lovely corridors – they are yours. Fill them with sweet echoes of dropping music; let the walls be covered with your works of art; let the girls laugh and the boys be happy within these walls. I give you the shell, the empty carcass; fill it with the spirit of content and happiness.

Where's Class War when you need them?

*

You could argue that J. G. Ballard's *High-Rise,* 1975, is a late-flowering variant of the slum novel. A forty-storey luxury tower block containing a thousand flats, located on the river two miles east of the City, starts out all squash games and cocktail parties, and ends up with the inhabitants separated into roaming gangs, passing the time with sex, violence and dog-eating.

Not that any of this would have affected the real-life Jim Ballard. He wouldn't have been seen dead in a tower block. Ballard said in a 2008 *Guardian* interview with James Campbell:

> I came to live in Shepperton in 1960. I thought the future isn't in the metropolitan areas of London. I want to go out to the new suburbs, near the film studios. This was the England I wanted to write about, because this was the new world that was emerging. No one in a novel by Virginia Woolf ever filled up the petrol tank of their car.

Incidentally, I'm not sure this is actually true. In *Mrs Dalloway,* Woolf's 'London walking novel', we have this sentence: 'The chauffeur, who had been opening something, turning something, shutting something, got on to the box.' That could be Virginia Woolf's notion of filling a petrol tank, couldn't it?

High-Rise confirms, though we probably knew it already, that slums are changeable and unstable places. They come and go. Once a slum isn't necessarily always a slum, and vice versa. Ernö Goldfinger's Trellick Tower, completed in 1972 – and Ballard's inspiration, by some accounts – was supposedly built out of socialist, utopian ideals, then rapidly deteriorated into a vertical slum; with lifts and garbage chutes that didn't work, it was beset by crime, drugs, violence, vandalism, all the usual problems found on 'bad estates'.

Gradually, Trellick Tower has been reclaimed, first by tenants who, under the Thatcherite 'right to buy' scheme, could see that owning a flat there might not be such a terrible deal after all, and subsequently by fans of Brutalist architecture. It has become a cool address that has little to do with Goldfinger's intentions.

Goldfinger was not so much a complainer as a shifter of blame. He insisted that none of the problems in the Trellick were caused by his design, but rather by others who failed to live up to his vision; notoriously, he was recorded as saying, 'I built skyscrapers for people to live in and now they have messed them up. Disgusting.' I suspect he's by no means the only architect to think this way, but he's one of the very few to say it.

Incidentally, Goldfinger did live for two months, on a sort of field expedition, in a flat on the twenty-fifth floor of the high-rise Balfron Tower, in Poplar, a project similar to the Trellick, built a few years earlier; then he returned to his house in Willow Road, Hampstead.

*

Which brings us to the four glass-and-steel towers of One Hyde Park, in Knightsbridge, designed by Richard Rogers, the polar opposite of the Trellick in many ways, and by most accounts the world's most expensive residential building. (There are some commercial enterprises in there too, including showrooms for Rolex and McLaren Automotive). At the time of writing, a three-bedroom apartment is for sale there at an asking price of eighteen and a half million pounds, but that's at the bargain basement end of things. One property (actually two apartments knocked together) was sold in 2010 for a hundred and fifty million – a world record of sorts – to Rinat Akhmetov, who's regularly described as 'the richest man in Ukraine', though evidently he's not in Ukraine all the time.

As a building, from the outside, One Hyde Park looks jazzy enough, without having the gob-smacking quality of much 'starchitecture', but it's hard to separate the aesthetic aspects from the symbolic. Peter York said of it, 'the vibe is junior Arab dictator', and Gavin Stamp called it 'a vulgar symbol of the hegemony of excessive wealth, an oversized gated community for people with more money than sense, arrogantly plonked down in the heart of London.'

The objection is not only about 'vulgar' displays and inequalities of wealth, though they are objectionable enough, but also that most of the flats in One Hyde Park are not even lived in. They're owned by dubious, shadowy offshore companies, and the human owners are genuine absentees. The properties are only incidentally places to live; in essence, they're markers, parts of diversified, international investment portfolios. Walk past the towers at night – nobody's home, the lights aren't even on: go pick the symbolic bones out of that one.

*

Those who know the history of Centre Point are not surprised that a building can become an emblem of an era and a political situation. Centre Point has always struck me as architecturally quite appealing, though Pevsner took a different view:

> The drooping arms of the cruciform precast concrete members which result in a remorseless horizontal zigzag across the sill zone is coarse in the extreme . . . The enormous supports at ground-level are no less

> coarse . . . There is a pool in front of that façade, with equally coarse shapes used for fountains. Who would want such a building as its image? It will have to be a company not only affluent but 'with it'.

And also, presumably, coarse.

But again, aesthetic considerations weren't really the issue. Centre Point was a speculative project, built by property developer Harry Hyams. It was completed in 1966 but stood empty for most of a decade, initially because Hyams wanted to find a single tenant for the whole building – which was the way he'd always done business – and later, such was the nature of rising property values in London at the time, it actually increased in value precisely because it was empty.

In January 1974 a loose coalition of squatter organisations, known as the Housing Action Group, briefly occupied the building as a protest against housing shortages in London, and by then Hyams was even getting flak from the government: Environment Secretary Peter Walker called it 'an incredible scandal'. Eventually Hyams relented and leased out the building floor by floor.

The story, naturally, does not end there. At the time of writing, Centre Point is being converted into eighty-two luxury flats – not in the One Hyde Park class but expensive enough, with prices starting at about a million pounds, though a five-bedroom duplex on the 33rd floor was said to be priced at fifty-five million. Thirteen 'affordable' housing units are included in the scheme.

*

In the 1960s, when William Burroughs arrived in the UK, usually coming in from Tangiers, and was asked by immigration officials the reason for his visit, he used to reply, 'Number One the food. Number Two the weather.' I'd have thought that was enough to get him bounced out of the country with 'undesirable alien' stamped on his passport, but perhaps the immigration people were immune to sarcasm back then. Burroughs was also, it seems, at least partly coming to London for the cheap housing.

Heathcote Williams, the playwright, poet, actor and activist, describes an encounter with Burroughs.

> I first met William Burroughs in 1963. I was working for the now-defunct literary magazine *Transatlantic Review* and we were planning to publish a piece of his called 'The Beginning is also the End'. I'd proposed doing a drawing of Burroughs for the cover and the editor of *TR* had agreed, and so I went round to see him in a tiny hotel room in Princes Square, Bayswater, which I gathered Alex Trocchi had found for him.
>
> Trocchi put his head round the door at some stage to check that the room was OK. I remember Trocchi saying, 'You can't go far wrong here, Bill, not at three pounds a week.' This was what the hotel cost, its being more like a run-down rooming house than a hotel.

'I think he found London bleak,' Williams adds.

In fact Burroughs was also in London to take the apomorphine cure for heroin addiction devised by Dr John Yerby Dent, and although he told Williams the cure was working, Williams observed that Burroughs was very keen on a cough mixture called Breathe-Eezee and J. Collis Browne's Mixture, a popular cure-all, both of which contained morphine and might have made him more tolerant of bleak surroundings.

Burroughs lived in London on and off between 1960 and 1974, experiencing both low and high life. After that cheap hotel in Bayswater there was another in Earls Court, but then there was a flat in Duke Street, St James's, off Piccadilly, around the corner from Fortnum and Mason. Maybe he liked the food there, after all.

But on balance he seems to have preferred the low life. In a conversation recorded over dinner with Barry Miles and Victor Bockris, he bemoaned the state of London.

> 'In the early sixties London was a very cheap, relaxed, and pleasant place to be. You could have a very good meal in a working-class restaurant for about three shillings.
>
> 'The Empress Hotel off the Old Brompton Road cost one pound a day with breakfast for a very good comfortable room. It [London] had been a pleasant place. It deteriorated rather shortly after that. The more positive times I had in London were in the early sixties . . . the Empress Hotel no longer exists. Nor do those cheap restaurants . . . Rents have quadrupled.'

Again with the food!

If this comes across as a very contemporary-sounding complaint, bear in mind that Burroughs was saying this in 1978. He also said that he occasionally went to pubs with Anthony Burgess. 'I asked him if he saw many other writers in London; he said, "No, they're all a bunch of swine." '

*

Heathcote Williams's own relationship with London extended both higher and lower than Burroughs's. The Eton-educated son of a Queen's Counsel, whose early plays were staged by the Royal Court Theatre (Angie Bowie appeared in *Remember The Truth Dentist*), he nevertheless embraced a kind of post-hippie, pre-punk anarchism. He was a graffiti-writer before it was cool, and he may well have been one of the people who made it cool. 'Use your birth certificate as a credit card' was one of his. He was an activist and provocateur who (with others) successfully sued David Holdsworth, the Chief Constable of Thames Valley Police after the force's violent clearing of the 1974 Windsor Pop Festival. He was also a kind of gig coordinator for an organisation called the Albion Free State Meat Frenzy.

However, his most conspicuous form of activism involved squatting. It would be vastly satisfying if he'd been one of the squatters at Centre Point, and maybe he was but I can't find proof. He was, however, definitely part of 'Rough Tough Cream Puff', a kind of estate agency, or at least information exchange, for squatters. The sign outside the door read 'established by Wat Tyler, 1381'. And if you think Burroughs's Bayswater hotel may have been bleak, trust me when I tell you that 1970s London squats could be a good deal bleaker.

Out of this activism Williams was eventually led to reject London altogether, at least symbolically, and form the Free and Independent State of Frestonia, a state within a state, which declared independence from Britain in 1977. This *terra nova* consisted of 1.8 acres in Notting Hill, a triangular lot bounded by Bramley Road, Shalfleet Drive and Freston Road; hence the name. One hundred and twenty squatters occupied buildings owned by the Greater London Council, which had plans to demolish them. This is a common enough London urge, to be within the city and yet somehow not part of it

This was politics as theatre and theatre as politics, which is not the worst form of either. Frestonia applied for membership of the United Nations, the Minister of State for Education was a two-year-old boy, and Williams was the ambassador to Great Britain. The hub of the state's recreational activities was the People's Hall where citizens watched *Passport to Pimlico* and footage of the Sex Pistols, two remarkably enduring poles of London subversion.

In recent years Williams has had a career as a reliably eccentric movie actor, not least playing a psychiatrist, Jacob Gerst, in *Basic Instinct 2.* It's a much maligned film and understandably so, but it does manage to create a gorgeously attractive London that looks simultaneously noir and hypermodern. The murderous heroine has an apartment in the Gherkin, a real-estate fantasy un-realisable in the 'real' London: nobody lives on that floor, it is reserved specifically for media shoots.

Williams was also briefly in the spotlight for writing –

or perhaps more properly compiling – *Boris Johnson: The Blond Beast of Brexit: A Study in Depravity*, a twenty-thousand-word 'collage' cataloguing the many failings and indiscretions of his fellow old-Etonian. These depravities ranged from being on the wrong side of the climate-change argument to referring to 'the chicks in the *GQ* expenses department'. He chose Johnson because he was the 'heaviest hitter' in the Brexit debate, and the work was widely described as a Swiftean satire. Williams's denunciation went the way of most satire and apparently made no difference whatsoever to the EU Referendum.

*

Like alienated father, like alienated biological son. In 2010 Heathcote Williams's son Charlie Gilmour, conceived by Polly Samson, and adopted by Dave Gilmour of Pink Floyd, was jailed for sixteen months (he served four) for violent disorder, after attacking a Topshop, standing on the bonnet of Prince Charles's car and hanging from a flag on the Cenotaph, all part of a protest against student tuition fees. The *Daily Mail* weighed in with, ' "Cenotaph rampage was down to rejection by my natural father": Charlie Gilmour's explanation for shameful behaviour at student riots' – though nowhere in the article was he quoted as saying these actual words.

Part of Gilmour's defence was that, as a student of history at Cambridge, he'd been studying the Captain Swing riots, and this education had given him ideas. Captain Swing was the fictional figurehead of protests by farm workers in 1830s, an essentially agrarian movement, although certain outliers had attacked Wellington's London house in his name.

Young Charlie did better once he got out of prison, working as freelance writer. He had a piece in the *Independent* – about squatting.

*

Prison has never been a very appealing option when it comes to finding accommodation in London, but as every piece of property becomes more valuable, as every area in the city becomes more desirable, a lot of people have noticed that the prisons in central London – Pentonville, Brixton, Wandsworth and Wormwood Scrubs especially – look like increasingly attractive bits of real estate. Her Majesty's Prison Service seems to be sitting on a gold mine.

At the same time, nobody denies that these prisons, built in the Victorian era, are in bad shape – decaying, dangerous, difficult to police, 'not fit for purpose' according to Lord Falconer. And so in 2015 Justice Secretary Michael Gove announced a prison-reform plan that envisaged building new prisons employing architects who would be 'able to design out the dark corners which too often facilitate violence and drug-taking'.

To achieve a violence-free and drug-free prison is no doubt a worthy ambition, although informed sources suggest that it isn't simply dark corners that facilitate drug-taking. Historically most drugs got into Wandsworth via prison visitors and the occasional 'throw over' of drugs hidden in pieces of rubbish or even inside the odd dead pigeon. But recently things have got a lot more high tech, and drones have been used as the delivery method. Ian Bickers, the Governor of Wandsworth, said, 'It shows people what my staff have to deal with on a day-to-day basis.' The staff are, of course, said to be 'demoralised'.

And staffing is another part of the problem, again linked to accommodation. Prisons are increasingly unable to find employees who can afford to live anywhere near these central-London prisons. The pay isn't great, considerably less than the thirty-thousand-pound London median salary, so of course the staff have to live in the outer reaches, from where commuting is expensive and, given the unsocial hours, sometimes impossible.

And so Gove announced a 'new for old' policy. Close down the old metropolitan Victorian hulks and build shiny new state-of-the-art prisons. I find myself envisaging that movie with Arnold Schwarzenegger and Sylvester Stallone, *Escape Plan,* 'No One Breaks Out Alone', though of course the notion is that these new prisons should be a kinder, gentler form of Panopticon, where prisoners could be rehabilitated and receive drug counselling.

Clearly the new prisons can't be built in the centre of the city, so why not build them on the outskirts, out where the staff already live? These new prisons would be financed by selling off the old ones – an opportunity to build three thousand new homes, according to Gove. But another problem immediately presents itself. You can see the appeal of a soulful conversion of a Victorian edifice that has retained much of its patina and some, but not all, of its penal history. But turning jail cells into luxury apartments will be, at the very least, bad PR. On the other hand, if the prisons are sold off for affordable housing, that won't raise enough money to finance the new prisons. No doubt we're talking about mixed use, but getting the mix right is going to be a very delicate process.

Still, whichever way it goes, the prisoners will be out at the periphery. True, it might be difficult for them to have visitors come all that way, and in fact there is something truly Victorian about this, a reminder of the time when mental asylums were built more than a half-day's travel from central London, so that the families of inmates couldn't get there and back in a day. But perhaps this won't be a problem. London Transport pushes its tendrils ever outwards, and, in any case, the families of prisoners surely won't be able to afford to live in central London very much longer.

FOUR

Some People

Only a damn fool would generalise about what a Londoner is or isn't, about what a Londoner does or doesn't do. But there are a lot of damn fools in the world, and while some of them know London pretty well, some of them don't seem to know it at all. Outsiders are quick to describe Londoners as arrogant, in too much of a hurry, rude, hostile, unwelcoming, cold, abusive, abrasive, potentially violent, smug, more concerned with style than substance, people with more money than sense. Five quid for a pint of lager, come on!

Some of this is debatable, though not all, and who could be bothered to debate it? In any case, none of it's news. Everybody has complaints about Londoners. Londoners have complaints about each other, which is to say they often have complaints about themselves. Sometimes the complaints don't seem strictly accurate.

In his memoirs, Giacomo Casanova writes of a visit he made to London in 1760:

> A man in court dress cannot walk the streets of London without being pelted with mud by the mob, while the gentlemen look on and laugh . . . They

> [Londoners] hoot the king and the royal family when they appear in public, and the consequence is that they are never seen, save on great occasions, when order is kept by hundreds of constables.

In *Around the World in Eighty Days,* published 1873, Jules Verne writes, 'English Phileas Fogg certainly was, though perhaps not a Londoner.' He goes on to describe why Fogg doesn't quality as a Londoner.

> He was never seen at the Stock Exchange, or at the Bank, or in the counting-rooms of the City; no ships ever came into London docks of which he was the owner; he had no public employment; he had never been entered at any of the Inns of Court, either at the Temple, or Lincoln's Inn, or Gray's Inn; nor had his voice ever resounded in the Court of Chancery, or in the Exchequer, or the Queen's Bench, or the Ecclesiastical Courts . . . His name was strange to the scientific and learned societies, and he never was known to take part in the sage deliberations of the Royal Society or the Royal Institution, the Working Men's Association . . . or the Institution of Arts and Sciences . . . He belonged, in fact, to none of the numerous societies which swarm in the English capital, from the Harmonic to that of the Entomologists, founded mainly for the purpose of abolishing pernicious insects.
>
> Phileas Fogg was a member of the Reform, and that was all.

It would be pointless, I suppose, to protest that by these standards very few people who live in London would merit the name of Londoner. Verne did visit London a couple of times, in 1859 and 1872, but I think you'd have to say he didn't quite get the hang of what a Londoner was.

In 1824, Thomas Carlyle, a Scotsman, wrote from London, where he was temporarily staying, in Southampton Street, Pentonville, to his brother Alick, back home:

> Of this enormous Babel of a place I can give you no account in writing: it is like the heart of all the universe; and the flood of human effort rolls out of it and into it with a violence that almost appals one's every sense . . .
>
> There is an excitement in all this, which is pleasant as a transitory feeling, but much against my taste as a permanent one. I had much rather visit London from time to time, than live in it. There is in fact no right life in it that I can find: the people are situated here like plants in a hot house, to which the quiet influences of sky and earth are never in their unadulterated state admitted . . . when you issue from your door, you are assailed by vast shoals of quacks, and showmen, and street-sweepers, and pickpockets, and mendicants of every degree and shape, all plying in noise or silent craft their several vocations, all in their hearts like 'lions ravening for their prey'. The blackguard population of the place is the most consummately blackguard of anything I ever saw.

Will it surprise you that just a decade later Carlyle and his wife Jane left their Scottish moorland home and moved to London? They rented a house in Cheyne Row, Chelsea, for thirty-five pounds a year, and became Londoners. In due course, having various complaints about the British Museum Library, not least that there were too many people using it, and he couldn't get a seat, Carlyle helped found the London Library. Not that becoming a Londoner made him regard London any more fondly. In an 1850 pamphlet titled 'The Present Time' he wrote,

> Thirty thousand wretched women, sunk in that putrefying well of abominations; they have oozed in upon London from the universal Stygian quagmire of British industrial life; are accumulated in the well of the concern to that extent. British charity is smitten to the heart at the laying bare of such a scene; passionately undertakes, by enormous subscription of money, or by other enormous effort, to redress that individual horror; as I and all men hope it may. But, alas, what next? This general well and cesspool once baled clean out today will begin before night to fill itself anew. The universal Stygian quagmire is still there; opulent in women ready to be ruined, and in men ready. Towards the same sad cesspool will these waste currents of human ruin ooze and gravitate as heretofore; except in draining the universal quagmire itself there is no remedy.

It would be nice to think that Londoners see their city

more clearly than outsiders, but as Carlyle shows above, a kind of lurid rhetoric sometimes takes over, and I'm not sure that they do. Here's Mary Gasalee, a character in Michael Moorcock's novel *Mother London*, recalling that the Blitz 'was the first time I fully understood how detached governments become from ordinary people. I never went home. I worked in the East End all that time. The carnage was disgusting. Expecting London to collapse, the authorities made no real provisions for defence. The ordinary people pulled the city through.'

This is suitably Bolshy but isn't it also sentimental? And Moorcock, born in Mitcham, which had been a London borough for five years at the time of his birth, displayed similar traits in a 2015 interview with Andrew Harrison, for the *New Statesman.* He recounted a recent visit to Notting Hill, a return to the place where he spent some of his best years.

He said:

> The place made me feel ill . . . it had become unbelievably horrible on every level. I mean, Notting Hill had been a place of horror and violence in the 1960s and 1970s. My mother daren't visit us. Next door was always knife fights and the police. But it was cheap and that's what you need as a writer with a young family. Now look at it. It's people in jodhpurs.

Yes, nostalgia for knife fights may be the sweetest nostalgia of all, especially if, like Moorcock, you were dividing your time between Bastrop, Texas and Paris, France, as he was at the time of the interview.

One beautifully acidic dissection of London nostalgia (at least I *think* that's what it is) can be found in Lionel Bart's song 'Fings Ain't Wot They Used T'Be'. The song is best known, if it's known at all any more, in Max Bygraves's benign and bowdlerised version, sufficiently sanitised to be sung at a Royal Command Performance. Lyrics run:

> There's Teds in drainpipe trousers and
> Debs in coffee houses and
> Things ain't what they used to be . . .

The original version appeared in 1959, in a production at Joan Littlewood's Theatre Workshop at the Theatre Royal, Stratford East. *Fings Ain't Wot They Used T'Be* was a mini-musical by Bart within a non-musical play by Frank Norman, and the equivalent lines read:

There's toffs wiv toffee noses and
Poofs in coffee 'ouses and
Fings ain't what they used t'be . . .

You may wonder how much, if any, irony there is in those lines, but Bart's intentions get a little clearer later in the song.

Once in golden days of yore,
Ponces killed a lazy whore
Fings ain't wot they used t'be . . .

Now, even if we're not quite of Lionel Bart's time, I think we can safely say he's not feeling entirely nostalgic for a time when lazy whores could be killed at the whim of their pimps. He seems to be implying it's *good* that things aren't the way they used to be. At least I hope that's what he's doing. In his other works, however, Bart's nostalgia seemed largely unironic: *Oliver* full of singing, dancing Londoners celebrating the joys of the workhouse and the jail; *Blitz* doing the same for wartime London.

Bart himself was an interesting case, a real Londoner to be sure. He grew up in Stepney where, by his own account, he entertained local street kids by making up rude words to popular songs. 'Every audience for one of my shows represents, to me, an extension of that gang of kids in the East End,' he said. Well, extension is a curious word to use.

After a number of hugely successful stage musicals and films, Bart bought himself a twenty-seven-room mansion, complete with a minstrels' gallery from which he sometimes watched the famous guests at his famous parties: the Beatles, Noël Coward and Princess Margaret sometimes put in appearances.

Bart may have grown up in the East End, but the mansion was in Chelsea. No doubt he felt nostalgic about Stepney and its salt-of-the-earth population, but he had no intention of living among them. Eventually he sold the Chelsea place and moved to a mews house in South Kensington. And after he'd gone bankrupt, and slid into alcoholism, he went to live in Acton.

*

Auberon Waugh isn't a writer you'd necessarily expect to understand this process of moving up and out, but one of his *Spectator* columns from April 1978, on the subject of punks, is surprisingly knowing. He writes:

> The interesting thing about Sid Vicious, Johnny Rotten, Victor Vomit and the rest of them is that they would probably agree with my thesis that one reason – not the only reason but possibly the main one – why these council estates are so terrible is because such horrible people inhabit them. 'We're ugly.' 'We're horrible.' 'We're evil,' they cry, and their desolation is compounded when former proletarian heroes – the Beatles, the Rolling Stones – betray them.

Rotten and Vicious were certainly Londoners. Johnny Rotten, *né* Lydon, was born in Holloway; Sid Vicious *né* John Simon Ritchie, was born in Lewisham. It's harder to say how much of a Londoner Auberon Waugh could claim to be. He was born at his grandparents' house at Pixton Park in Somerset, and lived most of his life in Combe Florey, also in Somerset. He did, however, have a London flat in Hammersmith (bought with the money from selling an ornate Victorian washstand, made by William Burges, which Sir John Betjeman had given Evelyn Waugh as a fiftieth-birthday present) and certainly spent plenty of time in London working for *Private Eye* and the *Literary Review*. I reckon that's good enough.

Waugh's ironies are so multidirectional that they often implode and self-sabotage, but he surely wasn't wrong about the betrayal that some people, not only punks, saw in the rock royalty who started out as authentic London lads, made a pile and then moved into their grand London mansions: Mick Jagger and Keith Richards from Dartford to Cheyne Walk, Jimmy Page from Heston to the Tower House in Holland Park, Pete Townsend from Chiswick to the Wick in Richmond. And a great many moved out of London, and indeed out of Britain altogether. Of course, nobody expected Mick and Keith to remain in Dartford, but some fans will always see the transformation from working musician to multi-millionaire as involving a loss of authenticity.

It might be hard to believe that Auberon Waugh and Sid Vicious inhabited the same planet, let alone the same city, but their co-existence demonstrates the absurdity of making any generalisations about what a Londoner is. Even so, magazines and websites are crammed with filler articles and clickbait with titles like – '10 Signs that You've Become a True Londoner', '8 Ways to Tell a Real Londoner from a Fake Londoner', '25 Things Only a True Londoner Would Know', 'Where Real Londoners Have Their Breakfast', and so on. The items in these listicles vary between the banal: true Londoners walk quickly, to the downright silly: real Londoners are consoled by the sound of sirens.

These two examples, and pretty much all the others on the lists, strike me as neither necessary nor sufficient in defining Londoners. I'd say there's no single defining feature that absolutely makes you a Londoner. On the other hand, it's always fun watching people trying to assert their London credentials, especially politicians, the kind of people who are always so eager to talk about 'ordinary' Londoners.

During the 2016 London mayoral election campaign, Zac Goldsmith (born in Westminster, raised in Ham, Richmond) was quizzed in the back of a black cab for the Victoria Derbyshire show, and demonstrated that he didn't know that Holborn is the next station after Tottenham Court Road heading east on the Central Line, nor that QPR play at Loftus Road. Does this mean that Goldsmith isn't a true Londoner? No, it means (what we knew all along) that he isn't much of a tube traveller or a football fan. You also got the feeling that he considered he was slumming even to be in a black cab.

To be fair, the election winner Sadiq Khan (born in Tooting, raised in Earlsfield) only did a little bit better at answering similar questions. On the other hand his manifesto was subtitled 'A Manifesto for All Londoners', thereby presumably including Londoners who are not true, not real and not ordinary.

*

Then there's the song,

> Maybe it's because I'm a Londoner,
> That I love London so.

That's a problematic lyric in all kinds of ways, isn't it? Loving a place simply because you happen to live there or happen to have been born there just doesn't seem like the very best reason. It's kind of like thinking Chelsea is the best football team in the world just because you happen to support it. (And, yes, Chelsea FC did release a singalong album in 1972, titled *Blue Is The Colour,* which featured a 'London Medley' that included 'Maybe It's Because I'm A Londoner'.) In any case, wouldn't it be better to love London because of its history, or its culture, or its pubs, or its opportunities for psychogeography, or in fact because of any quality inherent in the city itself, rather than because of some quality in you?

But perhaps we shouldn't be too hard on the song's composer and lyricist Hubert Gregg (1914–2004) who supposedly wrote it in twenty minutes and jotted it down on the back of a theatre programme. Gregg was indeed a Londoner, born in Islington, and eventually quite the showbiz polymath. He worked for the BBC from the 1930s onwards, was a composer, actor, novelist and director, not least of Agatha Christie's *The Mousetrap*: he called her a 'mean old bitch' in his memoirs.

During the war he served in the Lincolnshire Regiment, and while in London on leave he saw the ruin caused by doodlebugs, and was inspired to write the song. He intended it to be a wartime morale-booster but the song lay in hibernation until 1947 when the producer Jack Hylton asked if he had a song suitable for Bud Flanagan of the Crazy Gang. Gregg dug out the song, Flanagan liked it, and used it in the revue *Together Again* which ran for four years, making the song a classic.

Gregg had some experience with the problems of morale-boosting songs. In 1940 he composed 'I'm Going to Get Lit Up When The Lights Go Up In London', which again didn't see the light of day till a few years later. The song imagines and celebrates a time when the war, and in particular the blackout, is over, a time when Londoners will be able to get drunk as 'brightly' as they like.

> The whole ecstatic population will be canned,
> canned, canned,
> Thro' our gin and angosturas
> We'll see little pale pink Führers
> Hi-de-Heiling from the Circus to the Strand.

It's not Cole Porter but it's not half bad. And it was a controversial work in its way. Hermione Gingold (born in Maida Vale, much later the authoress of *How to Grow Old Disgracefully)* was offered the song, but she didn't want to sing it while there was still a chance the war might not be won by the Allies, and that the lights might never go up in London again. Nancy Astor, American-born MP for Plymouth Sutton, though the Astors owned a grand house in St James's Square, thought it was a terrible incitement to drunkenness, although as plenty of people might have told her, Londoners have never needed much incitement to get drunk, whether there's a war on or not.

However, once it looked as though the war was turning in Britain's favour the song became a hit for Alan Breeze, complete with cockney spoken-word elements (Breeze was born in West Ham). He says, 'Oh, Bill, what a night that's gonna be, eh? Can't you imagine that luverlee rosy glow all over town just like we used to see?'

The Bill he's addressing is Billy Cotton, another Londoner, born in Smith Square, Westminster in 1899, who had a career as a bandleader for the best part of fifty years, and made his last public appearance at a charity concert in March 1969 singing, of course, 'Maybe It's Because I'm A Londoner'. The following night he collapsed and died at a heavyweight boxing match at Wembley.

That is certainly one more version of what it might mean to be a Londoner, though some extraordinarily unlikely people have also sung that song – Davy Jones of the Monkees for one, Kirk Douglas for another. There is also a song from 2008 with the same title and some of the same lyrics, by a white London rapper named Hyperaptive. It includes the couplet:

> Maybe it's because I'm a Londoner
> People think I ain't a good lyric coungerer

No, I really don't think that's the reason.

*

The novelist Nick Sweeney tells the story of being in the French House pub in Soho, one night in 1986, and spotting an empty chair on which he promptly sat down.

In fact the chair 'belonged' to the artist Francis Bacon who had briefly vacated it and gone to the bar to buy a drink. Bacon's cronies were sitting nearby and didn't tell Sweeney it was Bacon's chair, presumably because they knew what was coming, and were about to enjoy it. In due course Bacon returned from the bar, but instead of saying the seat was his, and reclaiming it, he acted as though the chair was still empty and as if Sweeney didn't exist. He sat down on the occupied chair, on top of Sweeney, much to the amusement of the cronies. Sweeney managed to get out from under, his dignity in some disarray, but at least knowing that he'd got a Francis Bacon anecdote out of it.

Leaving aside the fact that Bacon was probably pleased to sit in a young man's lap, however briefly, the event demonstrates something crucial about a certain type of Londoner. He or she fails to acknowledge that other people, other *kinds* of people, even exist. Members of other tribes remain unreal and invisible.

Mind you, sometimes this seems preferable to the alternative, what we see so often in Londoners, asserting their group identity by complaining bitterly about all the other groups. Those living north of the river distrust those living to the south. Eastenders hate westenders. Nobody much likes Sloane Rangers, and everybody is supposed to despise hipsters and gentrifiers. Rival London football fans all hate each other, but sometimes certain groups come together to express hatred for Tottenham.

Snobberies and inverted snobberies abound, a notion well nailed in Will Self's short story 'The North London Book of the Dead'. The narrator finds that his dead mother is now living in Crouch End. He's understandably surprised by the fact she's somehow still alive, 'That and this business of living in Crouch End. Mother had always been such a crushing snob about where people lived in London: certain suburbs – such as Crouch End – were so incredibly non-U in Mother's book of form.'

*

OVER 50
For everyone over 60!
heer glossy 15 denier tights 95p.

So, are Londoners unfriendly? A lot of people complain that they are. In 2014 an organisation called 'Talk To Me London' got some headlines. They had a vision and a mission statement, of course they did. Their website said, 'We believe that through talking to strangers we can all help create a better world. We envision a world in which strangers feel comfortable striking up a conversation. Our mission is to change people's attitudes to talking to strangers and bring about more conversations between strangers in cities.' Originally participants wore badges to indicate they were part of the scheme, but later there were tickets which they handed to strangers they liked the look of.

There was a certain amount of predictable backlash – Londoners insisting that the attraction of living in London was that most people are strangers to each other, and want to stay that way. You don't know them and they don't know you, and you're delighted that you don't have to talk to each other.

It's hard to say how Quentin Crisp, the 'naked civil servant' who lived in London for more than forty years before moving to New York, would have felt about this. His exhibitionism guaranteed a good deal of public attention, and surely a good deal of conversation with strangers, but he did offer the opinion that, 'In London no one is your friend; in New York everyone is your friend.'

Where to start with that one? First perhaps by saying that if you meet somebody in New York who claims to be your friend, you'd better make sure that your money, credit cards and kidneys are somewhere safe. This applies in London, too, but as Crisp says, it rarely happens: because nobody would be stupid enough to fall for the kind of friendship that's offered too quickly or too easily.

The second thing to say is that to be everyone's friend is very much like being nobody's friend. London friendships require time, long acquaintance, discernment. What might look like coldness or standoffishness may in fact be respect. That's one explanation, anyway. But the truth is, not everybody *is* cold and standoffish. For every piece of anecdotal evidence of unfriendliness you can find an example of the opposite.

In the 2001 novel *Moon Over Soho*, by Ben Aaronovitch, a character says, 'My Dad says that being a Londoner has nothing to do with where you're born. He says that there are people who get off a jumbo jet at Heathrow, go through immigration waving any kind of passport, hop on the tube and by the time the train's pulled into Piccadilly Circus they've become a Londoner.'

That doesn't ring quite true to me. Neither does Peter Ackroyd's line in *London: A Biography,* in which he says 'It has often been remarked that in other cities, many years must pass before a foreigner is accepted; in London it takes as many months.' Remarked by whom? And what does it mean to be 'accepted'. Sometimes 'foreigners' are never accepted at all, though they can call themselves Londoners nevertheless.

Certainly there are plenty of Londoners, especially the newly arrived, who are looking for friends, but it's true that they often fail to find each other. The place is just too big and daunting and confusing. However, once provisional friendships have been established, people are often unhappy with the particular group of friends they have. They're looking for, perhaps believing they're entitled to, a better class of friend, something more rakish, more glamorous, more metropolitan.

Still, a city where you don't have friends, or have friends of the 'wrong' kind, can be a very lonely place, which brings us inevitably to Samuel Selvon's *The Lonely Londoners*. This short novel depicts working-class West Indian life in London in the 1950s. Selvon himself was considerably more sophisticated than the characters he writes about. He was a half-Indian, half-Scottish Trinidadian who lived in London for twenty-eight years, and worked for the Indian Embassy and the BBC. Still, nobody has ever accused him of being out of touch with the world he describes.

Some of the Londoners in Selvon's book seem a good deal lonelier than others; one of the characters, named Cap, hardly seems to be able to walk down the street without finding female company. And though they all have plenty to complain about in their new country – the weather, the casual racism of 'native' Londoners, their exploitation by landlords of their own race – none see themselves as victims.

Some of what the narrator describes is good old-fashioned, big-city alienation:

> It have people living in London who don't know what happening in the room next to them far more the street, or how the other people living. London is a

> place like that. It divide up in little worlds, and you stay in the world you belong to and you don't know anything about what happening in the other ones except what you read in the papers. Them rich people who does live in Belgravia and Knightsbridge and up in Hampstead and them other plush places, they would never believe what it like in a grim place like Harrow Road or Notting Hill.

Even so, with few exceptions, and although they have assimilated with varying degrees of success, Selvon's characters do think of themselves as Londoners, and they don't worry much about whether they're real or true or ordinary versions. Do they love London? Probably not, but they accept it and they continue to live there.

The book is written in what's been described as 'creolised English' but apart from some slang words and some non-standard grammar the language is completely comprehensible. Is language a determinant in defining your status as a Londoner? Scholars differ on the precise number, but it's probably safe to say that about three hundred different languages are spoken in London, which by some accounts makes it the world's most linguistically diverse city, although you can easily find claims that eight hundred different languages are spoken in New York. One assumes that linguistic diversity is a good thing, although an image of the tower hamlets of Babel does occasionally spring to mind, especially when we learn than more than three hundred thousand people living in London can't speak English well or at all.

At the 2014 UKIP spring conference (which was held in Torquay), the always jovial Nigel Farage said:

> I got the train the other night, it was rush hour, from Charing Cross, it was the stopper going out. We stopped at London Bridge, New Cross, Hither Green. It wasn't until after we got past Grove Park that I could actually hear English being audibly spoken in the carriage. Does that make me feel slightly awkward? Yes.

Of course, some of us think that anything that makes Nigel Farage feel awkward, or worse, is to be celebrated.

FIVE

A Bellyful of London

If you're going to complain about London, you're definitely going to complain about London food. Of course, many outsiders complain about *all* British food, condemning it simultaneously for its blandness *and* its strangeness, but London tends to get singled out. The non-British may not 'get' sausage rolls or Kendal Mint Cake, but they're *really* not going to get jellied eels or pie and mash with liquor. They're probably not going to enjoy Scotch eggs much either, invented by staff at Fortnum and Mason in the early eighteenth century, according to some accounts.

The Simpsons' Jack the Ripper, Tree House of Horror episode, itself a parody of Alan Moore's *From Hell*, puts the extreme view pretty well. The ripper here is the Muttonchop Murderer, thought at first to be Homer Simpson but eventually revealed as Chief Wiggum. He's caught because the handle of the murder weapon smells of eel pie, of which he's a big fan.

Apu	Please, I am not a killer, I am but a humble purveyor of disgusting British food. Head pudding, eel pies.
Wiggum	Eel pie, my favourite! We British sure eat crap.

That strikes me as a little harsher and less witty than we've come to expect from *The Simpsons*, but it's a common enough point of view. Is there any other city in the world that has a signature dish with the same name as a weather condition caused by pollution? London has: the London Particular, pea soup, the same colour as the green smog made up of natural and unnatural elements floating in the air in nineteenth-century London: Herman Melville may have invented the term. And as for 'pigeons in Pimlico', described by Hannah Glasse in *The Art of Cookery Made Plain and Simple*, 1747 – pigeons stuffed with mushrooms and truffles, rolled in a slice of veal and bacon, accompanied by filled puff-pastry patties – I'm sure many outsiders would complain about that dish if only they could find it on a menu.

The food of London is an obvious and easy target, but it's not a static one. As tastes and fashions change there are always brand new things to complain about. Take the Anglicised notion of fast food. Things were so bad in the late sixties and early seventies that the opening of the first McDonald's, in Powis Street, Woolwich, in November 1974, was regarded in many quarters as a cause for celebration. Until then Londoners had had to make do with the dire Wimpy Bar, its menu only slightly enlivened by the Bender, actually just a hot dog curled up to fit on a burger bun, but nevertheless the subject of much juvenile homophobic snickering.

McDonald's opened, and people rejoiced, at least until they'd made a couple of visits. When Margaret Thatcher attended the opening of a branch in her

Finchley constituency in 1983 she complained that the burger was so big that you needed two hands to eat it. But that was nothing compared to what became known as the McLibel trial.

Throughout the 1980s London Greenpeace (separate from the larger Greenpeace organisation) had denounced McDonald's for all the obvious reasons: exploiting workers, animals and children, damaging the environment, promoting an unhealthy diet. They produced leaflets with titles such as 'What's Wrong with McDonald's', and by 1990 McDonald's was fed up with it. They decided to take legal action, but London Greenpeace was an 'unincorporated association' without legal status, and so McDonald's served libel writs on five of the volunteers distributing the leaflets. Three of the volunteers apologised and went on their way, but two – Helen Steel and David Morris – fought the case and defended themselves in the UK High Court.

Proceedings lasted more than ten years, making this the longest-running case in English history. It's hard to say who won and who lost. The original judgment was largely in favour of McDonald's: Steel and Morris were found guilty of some of the libel charges, and ordered to pay £60,000 in damages, later reduced to £40,000, although both refused to pay. Further appeals tended to be in the pair's favour. Some sources say the case cost McDonald's £10 million, and it was generally seen as a corporate PR disaster. Still, given that McDonald's remains profitably in business, with two hundred and five branches in London alone, it doesn't seem a very decisive defeat.

Even though the McLibel trial took place in London, there's nothing uniquely London-centric in complaining about McDonald's. For a more direct and droll and sophisticated abuse of London cuisines, we could look to Stephen Sondheim's *The Ballad of Sweeney Todd*, first seen in 1979, and specifically to the song 'The Worst Pies in London', sung by Mrs Lovett, whose role was played equally convincingly by Angela Lansbury (born in Poplar or Regent's Park, depending on your source) and Helena Bonham Carter (born in Islington), and you can't say that about many roles. The lyrics, in part, run:

'Is that just disgusting? You have to concede it!
It's nothing but crusting! Here drink this, you'll need it!
The worst pies in London . . . '

The fact that Mrs Lovett is singing about pies she herself makes and sells to the public, captures the loathing of self and the contempt for customers that has historically been at the heart of the London 'hospitality' trade. This was exemplified by the staff of Wong Kei, a Chinese restaurant in Soho, who were so famously abusive that it became a house style and a bit of a joke, but you always felt they absolutely meant it.

*

You certainly don't have to be non-English to hate London food. In *The Expedition of Humphry Clinker,* Tobias Smollett's English provincial narrator writes, 'The bread I eat in London is a deleterious paste, mixed up with chalk, alum and bone-ashes, insipid to the taste, and destructive to the constitution. The good people are not ignorant of this adulteration; but they prefer it to wholesome bread because it is whiter than the meal of corn.' He's not very keen on the fish, poultry or meat either. 'As for the pork, it is an abominable carnivorous animal, fed with horse flesh and distillers' grains.' Pigs are surely omnivores rather than carnivores, and I can't help thinking that horse-fed pigs would taste, at the least, very *interesting*. As for the fruit, 'It was but yesterday that I saw a dirty barrow-bunter in the street, cleaning her dusty fruit with her own spittle.'

You may wonder whether it was always this way. The poem 'London Lickpenny', written in the fifteenth century, leaves the question open. It is narrated by a man from Kent who arrives in the big city and finds it all too much for him, not least the street vendors who are endlessly trying to sell him food. In this case his objection is to the hard sell and the expense rather than to the food itself; we don't get a report on the quality or cleanliness.

> 'Hot pescods!' one gan cry,
> 'Strabery rype, and chery in the ryse!'
> One bad me come nere and by some spice;
> Pepar and saffron they gan me bede,
> Clove, grayns, and flowre of rise.
> For lacke of money I myght not spede.
>
> Then come there one, and cried 'Hot shepes fete!'
> 'Risshes faire and grene,' an othar began to grete;
> Both melwell and makarell I gan mete,
> But for lacke of money I myght not spede.

Much probably depends on what you're used to. Many a foreign visitor to London might be prejudiced against sheep's feet and pescods (open-faced sweet mince tarts) but there's surely unlikely to be any real objection to strawberries or cherries.

According to Alan Davidson in *The Oxford Companion to Food*, the streets of sixteenth-century London echoed with cries of, 'Hot grey peas and a suck of bacon,' which even the dourest Londoner can't have found all that appetising.

*

Samuel Pepys (1633–1703) was a food lover, and a man who could be as enthusiastic about bread and cheese as he was about a slab of venison, but he was always especially happy with a barrel of oysters. By my calculations he mentions oysters eight-six times in the course of his diary. He was also, famously, enough of a gourmet to bury his wine and parmesan cheese to protect them from the Great Fire of London. He found much to enjoy about the food in London, but also found a few things to complain about.

In August 1667 Pepys and his wife went to Sir William Pen's house in Walthamstow, 'the first time I have been there, and there find him and all their guests . . . at dinner, which was a very bad dinner, and everything suitable, that I never knew people in my life, that make their flutter, that do things so meanly – I was sick to see it.'

One day in July 1660 he sent out his wife and his servant, Mrs Hunt, 'to buy something for supper; they bought a Quarter of Lamb, and so we ate it, but it was not half roasted.'

Undercooking was a recurring problem. In January 1661 he ate with a couple named the Pierces 'where we had a calf's head carboned, but it was raw – we could not eat it – and a good hen. But she [Mrs Pierce] is such a slut that I do not love her victuals.'

Even if the company was good, the food sometimes disagreed with him. On 25 January 1662 he had dinner with Sir William Rider: 'good cheer and discourse, but I eat a little too much beef, which made me sick, and so after dinner we went to the office, and there in a garden I went in the dark and vomited, whereby I did much ease my stomach.' Then he went out 'to supper with my wife to Sir W. Pen's'.

And on 19 June of that same year: 'to Moorefields, and walked and eat some cheese-cake and gammon of bacon, but when I was come home I was sick.'

And once in a while even his beloved oysters let him down. On 23 March 1662: 'And so home with Sir W. Batten, and there eat some boiled great oysters; and so home, and while I was at dinner with my wife, I was sick and was forced to vomit up my oysters again and then I was well.'

For a while anyway. Despite, or because of, Pepys's love of food, he had frequent stomach troubles. On 15 July 1666: ' . . . and so to bed in some pain and in fear of more, which accordingly I met with, for I was in mighty pain all night long of the winde griping of my belly and making of me shit often and vomit too, which is a thing not usual with me [we might beg to differ about that[, but this I impute to the milke that I drank after so much beer . . . '

Well, that's one explanation. Another might be that much of the food available in mid-seventeenth-century London required a stomach even stronger than Pepys's. It wasn't until the nineteenth century that reliable tests for food quality and safety became available, and they weren't exactly welcomed by food manufacturers.

In 1820, Frederick Accum published *A Treatise on Adulterations of Food and Culinary Poisons*: the title page shows a skull and the words 'There is death in the pot.'

Accum was a German chemist living in London: the book's dedication gives his address as Old Compton Street. It was, of course, already illegal in London, and anywhere else in Britain, to adulterate or misrepresent food products, but Accum's book detailed the tests to determine these things and his book revealed that just about anything that could be adulterated *was* being adulterated: beer, milk, bread, tea, coffee, sweets and jellies, and even medicines. More than that, he named the businesses involved.

He was duly hounded out of the country. The Royal Society accused him of tearing pages from books in their library, and he fled back to Germany rather than face the charges.

*

Do people complain more or less about food when there's a war on? More, I think. Food is a 'safe' thing to complain about. The rationing and scarcity of your favourite edibles are so much less troubling than the other things you have to worry about. Consider Ramos in Anthony Powell's *The Military Philosophers*:

> Ramos, in spectacles with a woollen scarf round his neck, looked a mild academic figure in spite of his military cap. He was obviously not at all well. The sudden impact of London wartime food – as well it might – had radically disordered his stomach. He had explained his case to me as soon as he arrived that morning, indicating this by gesture rather than words, his English being limited.

Evelyn Waugh, perhaps surprisingly, since we tend to think of him as quite the voluptuary, said in a preface to *Brideshead Revisited* that the book had been written in the last years of the war, 'a bleak period of present privation and threatening disaster – the period of soya beans and Basic English – and in consequence the book is infused with a kind of gluttony . . . which now with a full stomach I find distasteful.'

During the war, from 1940 onwards, communal kitchens were set up around Britain, named by Winston Churchill British Restaurants because that sounded considerably better than the original name of Community Feeding Centres. There were over two hundred of them in the capital, run by the London County Council, and they were more popular here than in the rest of the country.

They offered food that was cheap and simple, and people of all walks of life sat side by side, and although many of the British Restaurants were very basic, located in village halls and schools, others were in surprisingly swanky places like the banqueting hall of Gloucester House in Mayfair. But of course there were still reasons to complain.

In *London at War 1939–1945*, Philip Ziegler quotes from some wonderful manuscripts in the Imperial War Museum archive. Gladys Cox, who ate at a British Restaurant in the Finchley Road, found 'the clientele a mixed bag and service somewhat rough and ready . . . A navvy sat beside me in his working clothes.' And William Regan complained about the food itself: 'One potato, one piece of carrot and a 2" x 3" rectangle of boiled beef, followed by a small piece of boiled pudding, spoilt with evil-tasting sauce.'

*

One theory sometimes used to explain the low standard of London food sees purely practical reasons. As the city's population grew so rapidly in the nineteenth century, the demand for food far exceeded the supply. Barges and horse-drawn carts could only do so much to deliver to the city. Fresh food became scarce, and preservation became a necessity. Cooked meat in a pie lasted much longer than fresh meat. Jellied eels could last indefinitely. Root vegetables, far less perishable than their green equivalents, became much more prevalent. The theory then goes that by the time the supply chain was working properly, and good fresh food was again available, the London citizenry had simply lost the taste for it, or the knowledge of what good food was. I find myself not wholly convinced by this.

In any case, the taste for good food, and the ability to identify it, has supposedly come back with a vengeance in the last few decades, although you can't help thinking this may be a trend that people think they should latch on to, rather than being because they've suddenly developed exquisite palates. These developments have allowed a whole new group of people to complain about London food, not because it's low quality, but because it's so fancy and pretentious. The boozers are now all gastropubs, hot-beds of artisanal bar snacks and microbrewed IPA. Restaurants are all about palate-cleansers and lardo, morels and samphire, tasting menus and non-optional service charges.

*

There was surely never a time when people didn't share information about what was and wasn't a good place to buy or eat food in London, celebrating the good and especially complaining about the bad. Restaurant criticism is generally said to have begun in France with *L'Almanach des gourmands,* an annual publication that appeared from 1803 to 1812, written by Alexandre Balthazar Laurent Grimod de la Reynière, but England, and especially London, duly joined in.

Various guides to eating out in London appeared in the mid nineteenth century, an example being *London at Dinner: Where to Dine*, published in 1858, written anonymously. It's still a good read, full of general and specific advice about eating out in the capital, and generally positive and upbeat in tone, though naturally there are some complaints – about illumination, for instance. 'It is of the utmost importance that the dining-room should be well-lighted; this is a point often neglected at the tables of people who ought to know better, but are too indolent to give directions.'

The author is also concerned with the nature of menus:

> In ordering a dinner at a London tavern, at a suburban one, or a country inn, the bill of fare is the most misleading guide in the world. It usually contains seven or

> eight soups; fish plain and dressed in twenty ways; with every dish that the ingenuity of a man or woman can make out of beef, mutton, veal, and lamb – and in twenty-nine cases out of thirty it happens that what you particularly fancy out of the list is not to be had.

That sounds like a perfectly reasonable gripe.

Our man is also worried that London cuisine is being infiltrated and subverted by foreign influences: 'Leicester Square is the haunt of foreigners, and as they continue to frequent its restaurants, we must presume they are content with the fare provided for them. To English tastes they might not seem so satisfactory.' And later he writes:

> Strangers in London, with money at command to dine when, where, and how it may suit their fancy, can, with perseverance and tact, always gratify their propensities in reason, but we cannot undertake to direct the voluptuary where to pamper his palate and sow the seeds of wretchedness for himself. It is not in him to be satisfied anywhere. We address ourselves to the saner portion of society.

By the end of the nineteenth century Lieutenant Colonel Nathaniel Newnham-Davis had emerged as a great democratiser and demystifier of the London gastronomic scene. He wrote about food for the *Pall Mall Gazette*, and in 1899 published a restaurant guide titled *Dinners and Diners: Where and How to Dine in London*, which he updated two years later. In 1914 he published the

Gourmet's Guide to London. He claimed his audience was 'the Respectable Classes', and, as a former military man, he referred to himself as a 'soldier of the fork'.

Newnham-Davis isn't happy about the growing number of French restaurants in London, but he says that in general complaining isn't style. 'I prefer to consign to oblivion the stories I could tell of bad eggs and rank butter and cold potatoes, stringy meat and skeleton fowls. It is so much better for one's digestion to think of pleasant things than to brood over horrors.' This is a little frustrating, it leaves you wishing he'd complain a bit more, and let us savour the details of the failings of those terrible London restaurants he's been to, but perhaps I'm looking at this through contemporary eyes. Complaining about bad food has today become a rich source of entertainment.

*

The first modern English, and certainly London-based, food critic is generally reckoned to be Quentin Crewe – a journalistic all-rounder who was working at *Queen* magazine in the 1960s. The magazine usually featured a list of one-line descriptions of restaurants, but a day came when the woman who compiled the list was off sick, so there was a hole in the magazine. Crewe, who was about to go off for lunch at Wilton's, offered to fill the space by writing something about his experience there. The review was both witty and deeply insulting, with talk of nursery food served to aristos by waitresses dressed as nannies. It created something of a sensation, and it opened the floodgates for the likes of Clement

Freud, Craig Brown, Jonathan Meades, Giles Coren and AA Gill, all of whom have made at least part of their reputations by bad-mouthing bad London restaurants. It is, undoubtedly, a bit of a boys' club, though you definitely wouldn't want to get on the wrong side of Fay Maschler.

But the Torquemada of current London food critics is the gloriously vituperative Jay Rayner. Here he is writing about a restaurant called Novikov, just off Piccadilly: 'This is generally very, very bad: prices that knock the wind out of you and moments of cooking so cack-handed, so foul, so astoundingly grim you want to congratulate the kitchen on its incompetence.'

And here he is complaining about the restaurant Beast.

> You could easily respond to this week's restaurant with furious, spittle-flecked rage. You could rant about the posing-pouch stupidity of the meat-hanging cabinet that greets you as the lift doors open, and the frothing tanks of monstrous live Norwegian king crabs next to it, each four feet across. You could bang on about the bizarre pricing structure, and the vertiginous nature of those prices; about the rough-hewn communal tables that are so wide you can't sit opposite your dining companion because you wouldn't be able to hear each other . . . If Beast were a chap, he would be a part-time rugby player smelling of Ralgex who's trying to tell you he's deep and thoughtful, even though he'll later be implicated in an incident involving a traffic cone and a pint glass of his own urine.

Both Novikov and Beast are still in business at the

time of writing, which says much about the power of the press, and indicates that complaining often doesn't do any good, though no doubt it makes the complainer feel better. And these days all the amateurs are in on the act too, thanks to Yelp and Tripadviser. Here you will find essentially anonymous reviews from people you don't know, whose tastes you don't share and whose opinions you don't respect, but just occasionally the complaints soar into the realms of absurdist poetry.

'The grouse is just horrible and smells like poo.' That's a review by somebody called 'Pier 1'. This next one is from will D., Manhattan, NY:

> The food disgusted me. I got Bullets in my meat. I founds them on my mouse . . . It unacceptable. I told the restaurant manager but he won't say any sorry. He said, 'YOU CAN EAT THEM, NO PROBLEM.' He is a crazy . . . Really really discussing. NEVER AGAIN. Beside that, all the dishes I ordered, I could not eat it. It's kind of food for camping . . . very wild . . . way of cooking, looks like and taste . . . Also the restaurant has full of toilet smell, I am wondering why people not recognised this . . . Why this restaurant is so good? I don't get it. Anyway Never again. It's my nightmare.

Both these reviews are of Fergus Henderson's restaurant St John, which happens, in many opinions, including mine, to be one of the great restaurants in London; and it, too, has also somehow managed to survive these complaints.

*

Still, I think my favourite skewering (in at least two senses) of the London palate was written by Thomas Pynchon, who was very temporarily an inhabitant of London, though it's hard to think of him as a Londoner. It appears in the 'Disgusting English Candy Drill' section of *Gravity's Rainbow*. Tyrone Slothrop meets an old flame, 'an adorable tomato in a nurse uniform', named Darlene who takes him home to meet her landlady, Mrs Quoad. There he samples a variety of outrageous, though all too believable sweets, some of them pre-war, many of them homemade, most of them invented by the author.

Slothrop is fed with wine jellies, a marmalade surprise, a rhubarb cream, a gin marshmallow, something in the shape of a Mills bomb that, 'under its tamarind glaze . . . turns out to be luscious pepsin-flavoured nougat, chock-full of tangy candied cubeb berries, and a chewy camphor-gum centre. It is unspeakably awful.'

And at one point, because he's coughing so badly, he's given a Meggezone, 'the least believable of English coughdrops'. The taste

> is like being belted in the head with a Swiss Alp. Menthol icicles immediately begin to grow from the roof of Slothrop's mouth. Polar bears seek toenail-holds up the freezing frosty-grape alveolar clusters in his lungs. It hurts his teeth too much to breathe, even through his nose, even, necktie loosened, with his nose down inside the neck of his olive-drab T-shirt. Benzoin vapours seep into his brain. His head floats in a halo of ice.

So unbelievable does the Meggezone sound that I've met quite a few American readers who assumed this too was Pynchon's invention. It isn't. As somebody who grew up being given the occasional Meggezone for, I suppose, medical reasons I can swear that they were almost as dreadful as Pynchon makes them sound, though not nearly as much fun.

Meggezones were a London product, made by Meggeson and Co., based in New Church Street, Bermondsey. The street doesn't appear in the current *London A–Z*, and Meggezones are no longer produced. I'm not sure anybody has ever complained about that.

*

A strange, telling confluence of food, gentrification, pretension and class warfare came to a brief flood in September 2015 when the Cereal Killer Café in Brick Lane was attacked by demonstrators, variously described as anti-gentrification, anti-capitalist and anarchist.

Brick Lane, for decades a street of curry houses, where you might rough it in search of an authentic vindaloo, is now touted as a desirable area for up and coming financial whizz kids, the kind of people who wouldn't have been seen dead living there even a decade ago. Cereal Killer was, and remains, a prime example of the new wave of enterprises in the area, a twee little eatery selling breakfast cereal at what seem to most of us absurdly high prices: a hundred and twenty different brands, served with thirty kinds of milk and twenty toppings. Who knew there were thirty different kinds of milk?

On 26 September, an event known as the Fuck Parade, with profound ties to the anarchist group Class War, marched through parts of the East End. Their manifesto, zestily written, you'd probably have to admit, contained a denunciation of 'Russian oligarchs, Saudi sheiks, Israeli scumbag property developers, Texan oil-money twats and our own home-grown Eton toffs', and included the statement, 'We don't want luxury flats that no one can afford, we want genuinely affordable housing. We don't want pop-up gin bars or brioche buns – we want community.' No mention of breakfast cereal *per se*, though the manifesto continued, 'The past Fuck Parades have been fun and furious with music, pyrotechnics and cheeky banner drops.'

As the night of the demonstration wore on, the situation turned very 'cheeky' indeed. The whole 'parade' sounded ugly and threatening, and was meant to: it featured flaming torches and protestors in pig-head masks, fireworks were thrown and an estate agent's window was smashed, although in the end there was only one arrest. And at Cereal Killer paint was hurled at the café windows, somebody wrote 'scum' on the glass, and a smoke bomb was tossed into the doorway, though it only got as far as the foyer. Customers, eating cereal well into the evening, barricaded themselves inside, and nobody got hurt, but they were understandably frightened.

The owners of Cereal Killer, Gary and Alan Keery, certainly looked hipster enough – frosted hair, topiary beards, Alan with two sleeves of tattoos – although they described themselves as 'two working-class lads from Belfast'. Well, even working-class lads can be capitalists.

One of the brothers, news reports didn't make clear which, said, 'I can charge whatever I like. For the record, our bowls cost between £2.50 and £4.50. That is good value for a sit-down meal.' I'm not sure which is more surprising, that he thinks this is a reasonable price for a bowl of cereal, or that he thinks a bowl of cereal is a sit-down meal, but of course that may be the whole problem. At the very least it suggests that the Keerys and the participants in the Fuck Parade probably wouldn't be able to find much common ground.

Obviously there have always been tensions between rich and poor, but gentrification means the two are forced into very close proximity, and eating habits and eating establishments are a very minor but very conspicuous manifestation of disparities of income and lifestyle. In the end it was hard to pick a lovable dog in the fight between Cereal Killer and the Fuck Parade crowd. The café sounded pretty dreadful and absurd, but hardly the worst of the worst. The participants in the parade sounded like ill-intentioned troublemakers, but a bit of paint thrown on a window doesn't make them the worst of the worst either. Wouldn't a bad review on Yelp have been enough? Well no, evidently it would not.

SIX

And a Skinful

In 1902, Willa Cather visited London for the first time, and kept a diary, though it wasn't published until 1956, eight years after her death, as *Willa Cather in Europe: Her Own Story of Her First Journey*. She wasn't impressed by the city or the people, finding that:

> the streets are a restless, breathing, malodorous pageant of the seedy of all nations.
>
> But of all the shoddy foreigners one encounters, there are none so depressing as the London shoddy . . . Stop at any corner on the Strand at noon and you will see a bar, the street doors wide open, and a crowd of labouring men, red-faced and wet-eyed, pouring can after can of liquor down their throats . . . One cannot come to realise at once what an absolutely gin-soaked people these London working-folk are.

But one can realise it fairly soon.

*

London drinkers – so many to choose from, past and present, some real, some imaginary, some mythical – London drinkers like to complain, and they get complained about in return. There's Chaucer's London Cook, sozzled on his horse, and accused of being a lousy pie maker. Shakespeare has Falstaff complaining about the amount of lime in his sack, and being complained about by Prince Hal, 'The complaints I hear of thee are grievous.' There's Dickens's creation Krook, so hot with drink that he spontaneously combusts. There's William Nicholson's 'Sandwich-Man', one of the images in his *London Types* – the sandwich refers not to food but to the advertising boards he's carrying – and there's an accompanying poem by William Ernest Henley, which runs in part:

> The drunkard's mouth a-wash for
> something drinkable,
> The drunkard's eye alert for casual toppers,
> The drunkard's neck stooped to a lot scarce thinkable,
> A living crawling blazoning of Hot-Coppers,
> He trails his mildews towards a Kingdom-Come
> Compact of sausage-and-mash and two-o'rum!

There are the fictional inhabitants of Patrick Hamilton's *Hangover Square*. There was Nina Hamnett in the 1940s lurking in the pubs of Fitzrovia, more than willing to tell you all about her Bohemian exploits, so long as you kept her supplied with drink. Later there was Jeffrey Bernard who'd let you buy him a drink and then tell you to piss off.

Why do Londoners drink so much? Because life is hard? Because life is fun? Because there are so many places to get a drink – seven thousand pubs at a recent count. In the late sixteenth century one explanation attributed excessive drinking to the presence in London of Flemish pickled herrings, promoters of fierce and dangerous thirsts. Pickel Herring was the name given to an area of Southwark; it also became a generic name for a drunken clown. Pickled herrings are seen in the plays of Harvey, Rowlands, Dekker and Shakespeare. Toby Belch certainly consumes pickled herrings and complains about them when, 'half-drunk', he meets Olivia in *Twelfth Night.*

According to the Elizabethan scholar Gabriel Harvey, his hated rival Robert Greene died because of 'a surfeit of pickle herring and Rhenish wine'. Greene was the author of *A Groats-worth of Witte, bought with a million of Repentance* (1592), which contains what many have seen as an attack on Shakespeare, although it may have been written by his friends after his death. Greene in turn may have been a model for Shakespeare's Falstaff. Or he may not, such is the nature of Elizabethan scholarship.

*

Everything got much worse when gin arrived in London. The Glorious Revolution of 1688 put William of Orange on the throne, led to hostilities with France, outlawed the importation of French wine and brandy (although there were smugglers, naturally), and led to the 'Gin Craze', a state-assisted obsession with a specific kind of liquor that lasted sixty years or so.

Dutch connections encouraged the importation of gin from Holland, and in 1690 Parliament passed legislation to encourage the distillation of spirits made from corn, which also presented landowners with a new market and extra income. The whole nation took to gin happily enough, but Londoners took to it with a manic enthusiasm, and the city became a community of small-time distillers, gin sellers and gin drinkers.

There were few complaints at first – Daniel Defoe thought it was a very good thing – but as early as 1701 Charles Davenant, economist, Member of Parliament and originally a supporter of the new legislation, was already fretting about gin, ' 'Tis a growing fad among the common people and may in time prevail as much as opium with the Turks.' Within a few decades gin came to be seen as a major social evil, especially in London, and by then even Defoe had changed his mind. But as that quotation from Davenant shows, it was always the working classes who were seen as both victims and miscreants.

In 1736 a group of Middlesex magistrates stated:

> It is with the deepest concern your committee observe the strong Inclination of the inferior Sort of People to these destructive Liquors, and how surprisingly this Infection has spread within these few Years . . . it is scarce possible for Persons in low Life to go anywhere or to be anywhere without being drawn in to taste, and, by Degrees, to like and approve of this pernicious Liquor.

In 1735, in *A Trip Through the Town* – admittedly a scurrilous and moralistic publication, we find:

> The town of London is a kind of large forest of wild beasts where most of us range about at a venture, and are equally savage, and mutually destructive of one another. Observe the shops, and you'll see an universal discontent, and melancholy hanging in the faces of their respective occupiers.

Those shops were gin shops, although many were simply stalls or barrows. In 1730 there were seven thousand places to buy gin in London; ten years later there were nine thousand, for a population of less than seven hundred thousand.

1751 was a big year for the anti-gin lobby. Henry Fielding published *An Inquiry into the Causes of the Late Increase in Robbers*. Gin was the cause, obviously.

> Gin; which I have reason to think is the major Sustenance (if it can be so-called) of more than an hundred thousand People in this Metropolis. Many of these Wretches there are, who swallow Pints of this Poison within the Twenty-four Hours; the dreadful Effects of which I have the Misfortune every Day to see, and to smell too.

William Hogarth also got in on the act. 1751 was the year he issued his two famous prints *Beer Street* and *Gin Lane*: two imaginary streets but located in a recognisably real London. It's not hard to grasp the point. The folk in Beer Street are happy, healthy, industrious, prosperous, and they don't look drunk at all. In Gin Lane the buildings are collapsing, children are being neglected, boobs are out, the entire population is not simply drunk but looks thoroughly dissolute, on the edge of madness, starvation and suicide.

Although Hogarth's prints are generally described as satirical, it's not the most surprising kind of satire is it? The lower orders are unlikely to be moved to morality and sobriety by the sight of a print, and their betters don't need any reminding of the fecklessness of the lower orders.

There's also surely something jingoistic in the preference for native beer as opposed to 'foreign' liquor. And there's something patrician and perhaps misogynistic about the whole condemnation of the Gin Craze. Gin itself is personified as female, Mother's Ruin, Mother Geneva; but it also leads to a degree of emancipation, which in itself was seen as a problem in certain quarters; eighteenth-century gin palaces were the first places in England where men and women drank together, though that could also be condemned because it led women into licentious behaviour and turned them into bad mothers.

Perhaps legislation would succeed where art failed. Between 1729 and 1751 five major Acts of Parliament were passed in an attempt to control the production and consumption of gin. These acts generally involved duty and licensing. The 1736 Gin Act placed one pound of duty on every gallon of liquor spirit produced, and sellers needed an annual licence costing fifty pounds in order to sell it.

If obeyed, these measures would have effectively ended gin production in the whole of England, but nobody did obey them, only two licences were ever taken out and the trade went underground. There were a number of small scale Gin Riots, and in fact production and consumption of gin actually increased in the period immediately after the legislation was passed. Sources suggest that in 1736 eleven million gallons of gin were distilled in London; six years later production had risen by fifty per cent.

The Gin Craze declined after the passage of the 1751 Gin Act, which imposed rather more reasonable duties and licences, but at the same time the price of grain

The Drunkard's Cloak

also went up, and producing gin became a much more expensive business; the poor still wanted it but simply couldn't afford it.

Samuel Johnson had always been against punitive legislation where gin was concerned, partly on the demonstrable grounds that it was unenforceable. But more importantly he also believed that humanity needed all the comfort it could get. There is this passage in Hester Lynch Piozzi's *Anecdotes of the Late Samuel Johnson*:

> What signifies, says someone, giving halfpence to beggars? they only lay it out in gin or tobacco. And why should they be denied such sweeteners of their existence (says Johnson)? it is surely very savage to refuse them every possible avenue to pleasure, reckoned too coarse for our own acceptance. Life is a pill which none of us can bear to swallow without gilding; yet for the poor we delight in stripping it still barer, and are not ashamed to shew even visible displeasure if ever the bitter taste is taken from their mouths.

Elsewhere in the *Anecdotes* Mrs Piozzi's says of Johnson's drinking habits: 'His liking was for the strongest as it was not the flavour but the effect he sought for.' Even so, I can't find any hard evidence that Johnson himself was actually a gin drinker.

*

We know for certain that Gilbert and George, the 'Art for All' double act, the Flanagan and Allen of Fournier Street, Spitalfields, were, and very possibly still are, gin drinkers. The pair are not generally great complainers, though they're sometimes much complained against, and in general they're boosters for their own bit of London. George has said, more than once, 'Nothing happens in the world that doesn't happen in the East End,' though they can be a bit sniffy about other London areas. When asked in an interview with *Christie's Magazine* why they hadn't moved to Chelsea or Mayfair once they had the money, Gilbert said, 'It's dead down there . . . We feel the world here. We have to feel the world. Our emotions when we go for a walk in the street, what we feel, are so complex. It wouldn't be the same in Chelsea.'

Their link to gin was established in their 1972 video piece titled *Gordon's Gets Us Drunk.* Gordon's of course styles itself 'London Dry Gin' and was first produced in 1769 in a distillery in Southwark. Gilbert and George claimed they chose it because it was 'the best gin', though surely the double G was part of the attraction.

The twelve-minute video piece is a sort of human still life. A continuous shot from a static camera shows Gilbert and George sitting at a table in a ground-floor room in their house in Spitalfields. The light is murky, though the bright street outside the window is visible through net curtains. There's no reason to think they *aren't* drinking gin, but given the general gloom and low quality of the video, they could be drinking anything at all. For that matter it's hard to see whether or not they're actually drunk, though a dubbed voice over on the soundtrack has a voice (George's according to the Tate catalogue) repeating variations on the phrase, 'Gordon's makes us very, very drunk.' There's music on the soundtrack too, Grieg and Elgar, including 'Land of Hope and Glory'.

Gilbert and George claimed that the piece 'deals with the ecstasy and intellectuality of legalised euphoria' and some have seen it as a kind of subversive, perhaps Warholian, commercial; it definitely does make you feel like having a drink.

But gin wasn't the only tipple for Gilbert and George. According to archive material uncovered by the *Art Newspaper* there was a glorious occasion in 1974 when the two artists were taken out to lunch by Tate Gallery curators, including Anne d'Offay, wife of the art dealer Anthony d'Offay. According to the expenses claim, the two Spitalfields lads drank 'the majority' of three bottles of wine and 12 glasses of vintage port. The implication seems to be that the Tate flunkies were moderate in their consumption. In any case, they directed all the blame on to the artists.

The alcohol consumption was no doubt excessive, but it's still surprising that, as the documents claim, the bill for the meal accounted for eight per cent of the Tate's annual entertainment budget: the wine and port must have been pretty decent. When the expenses claim was queried, Anne d'Offay replied, 'Unfortunately, Gilbert and George consumed an astronomical amount of drink . . . You can imagine that it was impossible to stop them ordering without creating a rumpus. By continuous questioning under the guise of hospitality we extracted a good deal of important information.'

Well, the powers that be weren't having that. Peter

O'Donohoe, a senior executive officer (whatever that might involve at an art gallery), wrote in a memo in reply to Anne d'Offay, 'I find it difficult and alarming to believe that the only way of obtaining information . . . from these artists was allowing them to become intoxicated . . . I would be very loath to put much credence on anything said that was alcohol assisted.' He had a point, but the way he writes, you'd think he'd never met an artist. They have been known to like a drink; in London as everywhere else.

*

In a 2001 review in the *Guardian* of an exhibition titled The Urethra Postcard Art of Gilbert and George, Jonathan Jones wrote, 'A urethra, a conduit through which everything comes flooding out – that's what Gilbert and George have provided throughout their shared career. Living in East London, they are the city's living sewer – and I mean that as praise.'

Just about every term in those two sentences is debatable, including the nature of a sewer, the function of the urethra, the definition of 'everything' and the definition of 'flood'. Still, when it comes to alcohol, not all floods are metaphoric.

In 1814, the Meux Brewery stood in Tottenham Court Road, part of the St Giles Rookery, a slightly different part from the one whose inhabitants wrote the famous letter of complaint to *The Times*, but still within that parish which, according to Henry Mayhew, because of its 'nests of close and narrow alleys and courts inhabited by the lowest class of Irish costermongers, has passed into a byword as the synonym of filth and squalor'.

The brewery was by no means London's biggest, but it was a considerable enterprise, producing over a hundred thousand barrels of porter a year, so that at any given moment there were vast quantities of beer on the premises in various stages of fermentation and ageing. On the afternoon of 17 October 1814, at about half past four, George Crick, a storehouse clerk, inspected one of the twenty-foot-tall wooden vats containing half-fermented porter, and saw that one of the metal hoops holding it together had slipped. This kind of thing happened once in a while apparently, and although Crick reported it, as was his duty, neither he nor his immediate boss thought it needed urgent attention.

About an hour later the vat exploded, releasing a hundred and thirty-five thousand gallons of porter. The flying debris smashed open other nearby vats, so that eventually over three hundred thousand gallons of beer were liberated. Walls collapsed in the torrent, brickwork went flying into the world outside, but, incredibly, none of the workers in the brewery was killed. Outside, however, it was a difference story.

A tidal wave of beer, waist-deep in places, gushed through the badly drained neighbouring streets, pouring into dwellings, causing destruction as it went. Behind the Tavistock Arms in Great Russell Street, a fourteen-year-old servant girl named Eleanor Cooper was killed when a wall collapsed on her. In a tenement in New Street, Mary Banfield was having tea with her four-year-old daughter.

Beer swept into the room, carried the child away and drowned her. At the Ship in Bainbridge Street, Anne Saville was attending the wake of her two-year-old son who'd died the previous day: the flood killed her and five other mourners.

The London-based *Morning Post*, reported that the scene around the brewery was like the aftermath of an earthquake. 'To those that even approached the scene of ruin, the fumes of the beer were very offensive and overpowering.' Elsewhere the *Bury and Norfolk Post* reported:

> When the beer began to flow, the neighbourhood, consisting of the lower classes of the Irish, were busily employed in putting in their claim to a share, and every vessel, from a kettle to a cask, was put into requisition, and many of them were seen enjoying themselves at the expense of the proprietors.

This doesn't sound altogether unlikely but there are no other reports of it happening, which suggests it may have been motivated by anti-Irish sentiment.

Improbably found floating in the beer flood were parts of a domestic still: apparently somebody in the neighbourhood had been illegally distilling gin.

Two days after the flood, a jury was assembled to consider the case. They visited the site, viewed the dead bodies, heard evidence from eyewitnesses – George Crick seems to have acquitted himself pretty well – and concluded that the tragedy was an 'Act of God'. No point complaining to him.

SEVEN

Some Disorders

Did the Clash really want a riot, a white riot, a riot of their own? Well, if you listen to the lyrics of their song 'White Riot' you could be forgiven for thinking so. The song is attributed to Joe Strummer and Mick Jones, although apparently it was written after Strummer and bass player Paul Simonon had been involved in riots at the 1976 Notting Hill Carnival.

They were willing participants at first but, according to Simonon, at a certain point they concluded that this wasn't their fight. This was a 'black riot' in response to racist policing. As a couple of middle-class white boys, Strummer and Simonon didn't feel entitled to join in: a subtle and really quite touching response.

The song came shortly after. According to other post-factum interviews, it was not so much intended as a call to the barricades for disaffected white kids, much less as a demand for a race war – as it was perceived in certain idiotic quarters – but in fact as a bit of wishful thinking, hoping those disaffected white kids would develop political consciousness, mobilise themselves and decide they had a cause worth fighting, and rioting, for. Other interpretations are no doubt possible.

The lyrics in part run:

> Black man gotta lotta problems
> But they don't mind throwing a brick
> White people go to school
> Where they teach you how to be thick.

Which is a bit little less subtle and touching, if you ask me.

*

There's something very familiar about the London life of Joe Strummer. He was the public-school-educated son of a career diplomat, so of course he 'rebelled' – as an art student, as a busker, a squatter in Maida Vale, a pub rocker who morphed into a punk, and at one time a council-flat dweller on the World's End Estate in Chelsea where he wrote 'London Calling'. He was a man who sang that he wanted a riot, and in due course sent his daughter to Bedales, and eventually moved out of London to a 'very nice house in the country'.

We shouldn't be wholly surprised that the Clash make an appearance in Tony Benn's diaries. He writes on Wednesday, 28 December 1977:

> I rang the manager of the Clash, a political punk-rock group, because there had been a suggestion from the BBC Television Community Programme Unit that I have a four-minute discussion with the group. I had grave doubts about a Cabinet Minister appearing with a punk-rock group, given what the media would make of it, and he agreed with me that four minutes was not

> enough for a serious discussion. But what he said was interesting. The Clash are apparently very popular with working-class youngsters who don't find anything in our popular culture that meets their needs or reflects their feelings. He told me the group were not really concerned with being commercial and refused a lot of television because it put them into an artificial setting when they were really a live group. . . He said that to get any attention at all you had to be absolutely bizarre, but to understand what the Clash were trying to say you had to work really hard because the lyrics were in pidgin French.

At the time, the manager of the Clash would have been Bernie Rhodes, a Stepney lad, raised in an orphanage, who presumably was having a laugh at the expense of the born-with-a-title, Holland Park-dwelling Benn. Had Benn never actually heard the Clash? Or had he heard them and thought they really might be singing in pidgin French? It seems a plausible and forgivable mistake. It seems a bit less forgivable to refer to 'working-class youngsters'.

Is there some inescapable connection between London rock music and London riot? It's not hard to make the case. They both certainly stir up the blood, and although of course we're well aware of Riot Girls and Pussy Riot, both rock music and riot tend to be the preserve of testosterone-fuelled young men. As Simon Reynolds and Joy Press write in *The Sex Revolts*: '. . . the Clash's songs ache with a lust for glory and are riddled with highly charged militaristic imagery . . . The real object of the Clash's ardour is the bliss of boyish camaraderie, the potency of a strength in numbers that falls midway between the teenage gang and the militaristic formation.' It might also be said that those black rioters in Notting Hill in 1976, the ones Simonon and Strummer decided not to join in with, were more likely to be listening to reggae than rock, much less punk, though in due course the Clash covered that base too.

*

Less than a decade earlier it had seemed, as Mick Jagger put it, that in sleepy London town there was just no place for a street-fighting man. And he had a point. Compared with what was happening in Europe and the United States in the middle to late 1960s, events in London might well have seemed tame. London students were not acting up the way their Parisian counterparts were. There were no British troops in Vietnam, and although many British people were against the war there, in some way it didn't feel like 'our fight'.

Even so, on 17 March 1968 a vast crowd of demonstrators congregated in Trafalgar Square to protest against the war in Vietnam. Tariq Ali and Vanessa Redgrave were there (both wearing headbands) and so was Mick Jagger. Estimates of the size of the crowd vary wildly, and seem to have risen over the years. At the time, the *Guardian* estimated the crowd at thirty thousand, but in subsequent retellings the highest estimates put it at eighty thousand, though it's hard to see how that many people could ever have fitted into Trafalgar Square.

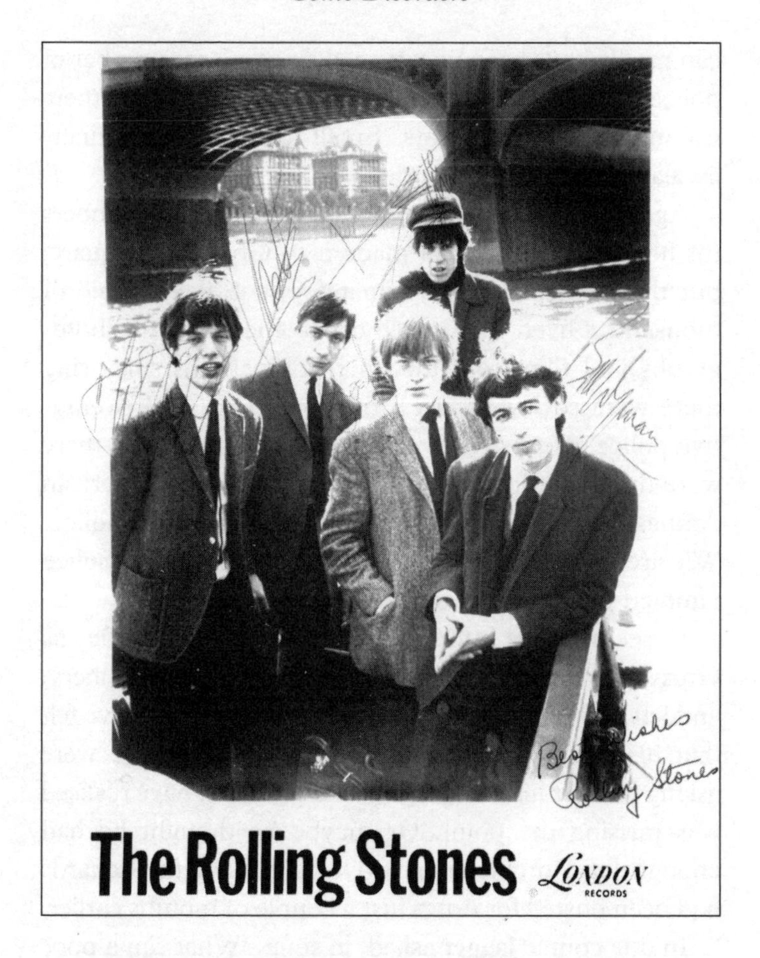

Speeches were made and then the crowd was due to march to Hyde Park, which the vast majority did, but at some point a breakaway group (which may well have been urged on by militant factions: anarchists, Maoists, skinheads have all been accused) headed for Grosvenor Square, site of the United States Embassy. This detour can hardly have been unexpected since a large number of police, some mounted on horseback, were already there waiting for the protestors. Small skirmishes eventually escalated into a full-scale riot.

Again it's difficult to come up with reliable numbers for how many protesters made it to Grosvenor Square, but the most plausible estimates put it at a couple of thousand. Given the degree of violence seen in photographs and film from the time, it's perhaps surprising there were so few injuries: fifty protesters and twenty-five police officers received hospital treatment and there were three hundred arrests. David Bruce, the American Ambassador, issued a statement thanking the police. 'We are most grateful for the magnificent way the police handled the attack on the Embassy.'

It seems that Mick Jagger did make it as far as Grosvenor Square, though he stayed on the periphery, and left before things turned really ugly. He may have felt that his pop-star status was a distraction: people were asking him for his autograph, which he must have realised was missing the point. Or maybe he thought he had enough legal problems already: he and Keith Richards had been busted for drugs just a couple of months earlier.

In due course Jagger asked, in song, 'What can a poor boy do but sing in a rock 'n' roll band?' There's some irony in that use of the word 'poor', no doubt. In May 1968 Jagger bought a house in Cheyne Walk, not exactly the address of a poor boy, much less of a street-fighting man.

There are plenty of first-hand accounts of the events

in Grosvenor Square that day, but perhaps the most surprising comes from Peter Hitchens, the author and journalist who has described himself as a 'Burkean conservative', and who wrote in the *Mail on Sunday* in January 2008:

> Very soon it will be the fortieth anniversary of the day I threw lumps of mud at the police in central London. I had precious little idea why I was doing it, though I can confirm that riots are fun for those who take part in them, and that rioters usually riot because they enjoy it.
>
> I wasn't oppressed, deprived, abused, underprivileged, poor or any of the other things people give as justifications for this sort of oafishness. I had no excuse then, and offer none now. I was a self-righteous, arrogant, spoiled teenage prig, and yes, I know quite a lot of people think I am still more or less the same, only middle-aged.

An impressive bit of self-knowledge there, though it leaves open the question of whether he thinks there are *any* justifiable grounds for rioting. Many of us might think that oppression, deprivation, abuse, underprivilege and poverty are perfectly good reasons for rioting. Though, perhaps, this is only to say that some riots seem more reasonable than others; just like some complaints.

*

There's a widespread and comforting belief that rioting is the means by which the powerless and marginalised find a voice and express themselves in the only way open to them. This is, of course, sometimes true, but not always. There are also occasions when the powerless and marginalised are on the receiving end from those who have more power than they do.

In 1189, after the coronation of Richard I, who had forbidden Jews (and indeed women) to attend the ceremony, a rumour spread through London that the king had ordered all Jews to be killed. A rumour was all that was needed. Jews were robbed, murdered, burned alive in their own homes and sometimes baptised by force. The last of these seems by far the most attractive option.

It remains unclear whether Richard actually *had* ordered the killing of Jews: the contemporary historian Roger of Howeden said it was all done by 'prejudiced and bigoted citizens', which seems undeniable. He also said that Richard punished the worst of the rioters and murderers. However, since Howeden went on the Third Crusade with Richard, he may have had a vested interest in showing the king in a good light.

The Evil May Day riots of 1517 weren't much more forgivable, though a good deal less deadly. 'Native' Londoners protested that there were too many 'foreigners' in the city. A thousand or so labourers – apprentices, Thames watermen and city porters – gathered in Cheapside and went through the City of London looting and destroying any property they happened to think belonged to foreigners. This time French immigrants were the prime target, although Jews and the Dutch also suffered. It was the biggest civil disturbance London had seen up to that time, many were injured, and thousands of troops were sent in to control the riot, but it seems that nobody died in the riot itself. Thirteen of the rioters were, however, subsequently executed for treason.

Twenty-year-old Edward Hall was an eyewitness. He wrote of the prevailing conditions:

> The multitude of strangers was so great about London that the poor English could scarce get any living . . . The foreigners . . . were so proud that they disdained, mocked, and oppressed the Englishmen, which was the beginning of the grudge . . . The Genoans, Frenchmen, and other strangers . . . boasted themselves to be in such favour with the king and his council that they set naught by the rulers of the city . . . How miserably the common artificers lived, and scarcely could get any work to find them, their wives, and children, for there were such a number of artificers strangers that took away all the living in manner.

If this sounds like xenophobic ranting, and it kind of does, it should be noted that Edward Hall went on to become a Member of Parliament, a friend of Thomas Cromwell, and eventually Under Sheriff of London.

The Gordon Riots of 1780 were in response to the Papist Act, passed two years earlier, repealing official discrimination against Catholics. Some folks didn't like that; they *wanted* Catholics to be discriminated against. There were attacks on the houses of both rich and poor Catholics, on the Bank of England, as well as the Clink and Newgate Prison, and at the last of these the words 'His Majesty King Mob' were daubed on the wall, thereby personifying the violent underbelly of London, as well as providing a character for Alan Moore and Grant Morrison two hundred years later, though it's hard to feel unalloyed admiration for the rioters of 1780.

For that matter it's hard not to feel some ambivalence about the 1990 Poll Tax Riots. In a way they seemed all too predictable. There had been a previous spot of bother about a poll tax in 1381 with the Peasants' Revolt and Wat Tyler, 'the first English revolutionary'. The 1990 poll tax was massively unpopular, and a protest seemed utterly reasonable, but if you had happened to be in the vicinity of the Strand or Covent Garden on the afternoon of 31 March as looters smashed shop windows and attempts were made to set fire to the South African Embassy, you might have thought the protests had lost much of their credibility. Tony Benn had been in Trafalgar Square and told the crowd they'd made their point and should all disperse quietly. On the other hand, the poll tax was duly abandoned and that defeat was at least partially responsible for Margaret Thatcher's downfall. It's an ill riot that blows nobody any good.

*

The riot most of us can unreservedly get behind is the one that took place in the East End of London on Sunday, 4 October 1936, now known as the Battle of Cable Street. It was a 'battle' widely perceived as a noble, and (more importantly) successful, attempt to confront Oswald Mosley and his British Union of Fascists, and prevent them marching through Shoreditch, Limehouse,

Bow and Bethnal Green. It would be nice to believe this was a spontaneous act of solidarity from the local community, but undoubtedly outsiders were involved. Plans for the march were well known in advance, and the Communist Party, led by Phil Piratin (later an MP), was certainly involved in organising the protest.

At the same time, the Jewish Board of Deputies advised Jews to keep away. The *Jewish Chronicle* wrote: 'Jews are urgently warned to keep away from the route of the Blackshirt march and from their meetings . . . Jews who, however innocently, become involved in any possible disorders will be actively helping anti-Semitism and Jew-baiting. Unless you want to help the Jew baiters, keep away.' Some may have, but many did not.

As ever, estimating the numbers involved is a hit-and-miss affair. It seems reasonable to believe there were at least a hundred thousand anti-Mosley protestors, though some estimates rise to a quarter of a million. Clearly not every one of these was a local, but equally they can't all have been agitators shipped in from outside.

Estimates of the number of Mosley supporters are equally wide ranging, from one thousand to five thousand. And between these two opposing groups there were (a more generally agreed upon figure) six thousand police. The man in charge of controlling the crowds, Metropolitan Police Commissioner Sir Philip Game, was clearly between a rock and a hard place. He had to show that the police remained in control of London, and that its streets did not belong exclusively to political factions of whatever ideology. This of course put him in the invidious position of defending Mosley and putting his men at risk as a buffer between warring groups, and ultimately as the focus of anti-fascist anger. In the end it was not a battle between fascists and anti-fascists but between anti-fascists and police.

Sir Philip Game could be said to have failed to control the streets of the East End, even if we happen to like the result that this thwarted Mosley. At about five o'clock that afternoon, after a three-hour pitched battle, he told Mosley he could no longer guarantee the safety of his supporters. 'If you go ahead, sir, it will be a shambles!' he's supposed to have said.

Mosley must surely have realised by then that numbers were not on his side, and he accepted the inevitable. He took his supporters back to Charing Cross and delivered a final speech saying, 'The Government surrenders to

Red violence and Jewish corruption. We never surrender. We shall triumph over the parties of corruption because our faith is greater than their faith, our will is stronger than their will.' The London District Committee of the Communist Party declared, 'This is the most humiliating defeat ever suffered by any figure in English politics.' Neither of these statements strikes me as essentially true.

There's some evidence that events in Cable Street actually strengthened Mosley's support, at least temporarily, although this was certainly a turning point, and it remains a symbolic landmark in confronting and vanquishing fascism. The government played its part too. It passed the Public Order Act of 1936, which required police consent for political marches, and declared illegal the wearing of political uniforms in public.

Mosley was also overtaken by events. When war broke out the British Government passed Defence Regulation B which allowed the Home Secretary to suspend habeas corpus and imprison anyone thought likely to 'endanger the safety of the realm'. By 1940 Mosley was in jail, in Brixton.

His wife Diana Mitford was also interned, although after Churchill's intervention they spent several years living together in a house in the grounds of Holloway, employing fellow prisoners as domestic help. This looked like, and was, special treatment. The prison priest is supposed to have complained to the warden: 'It's the Garden of Eden out there, Lady Mosley in her little knickers.'

They were released, in November 1943, amid widespread protests, and Diana's sister, Jessica Mitford, described the decision as 'a slap in the face of anti-fascists in every country and a direct betrayal of those who have died for the cause of anti-fascism', which even allowing for sisterly rivalry seems something of an exaggeration.

Perhaps tired of London, or perhaps tired of life, the released pair went first to stay with Pamela Mitford in Hampshire, and then bought Crux Easton House, in Berkshire, where they stayed under house arrest for the remainder of the war.

*

Perhaps the most intriguing and perplexing of London's civil disturbances were the Brown Dog Riots of 1907. On 10 December of that year, a group of medical students gathered in Battersea to topple a drinking fountain which had a statue of a dog at its summit. It was the inscription that really had the students riled. It read:

> In Memory of the Brown Terrier Dog Done to Death in the Laboratories of University College in February 1903 after having endured Vivisections extending over more than two months and having been handed over from one Vivisector to another till Death came to his release. Also in memory of the 232 dogs vivisected in the same place during the year 1902. Men and Women of England, How long shall these Things be?

The medical students didn't like that: yes, they were rioting in favour of vivisection.

They failed to topple the statue because they were chased off by a loose coalition of locals and political activists, and no doubt by people who simply didn't like students. The students then made a half-hearted and unsuccessful attempt to storm the nearby Anti-Vivisection Hospital, and then they moved on to Trafalgar Square, where else? By then their numbers had grown to two or three thousand, by some accounts, and there they clashed with police, as well as their Battersea opponents who had pursued them. It was a curious antagonism between science and sentiment, between compassion and the arrogance of the old-school medical establishment, an antagonism that still seems very modern. Feminism was in the mix too.

Things had started in 1903 when two Swedish female activists named Lizzy Lind af Hageby and Leisa Katherine Schartau enrolled at University College so they could witness vivisection at first hand. In due course they attended a lecture and demonstration in the physiology department, where William Bayliss was performing an operation on a brown terrier. Bayliss was doing important work on hormones and the pancreas, and he was licensed to perform vivisection, which was legal within the bounds of animal-cruelty legislation.

Nevertheless, the experiment does sound unnecessarily gruesome in the women's account. The dog, which had been operated on before (a breach of regulations in itself, though it would have been considered only a minor one), was tied to a board, cut open, and after the demonstration killed with a knife through the heart. More than that, af Hageby and Schartau claimed the dog was awake, twitching and visibly in pain throughout the procedure. Bayliss, backed up by his students, insisted the dog had been properly anaesthetised.

The women showed a diary account of the episode to Stephen Coleridge (some distant kin of Samuel Taylor), secretary of the National Anti-Vivisection Society. Shortly thereafter he repeated the information in a speech at the annual meeting of the National Anti-Vivisection Society. Details of the speech were published the next day in the *Daily News*, causing a lot of bad publicity for Bayliss, who demanded a public apology. Coleridge refused to give one, and Bayliss sued for defamation. The jury took twenty-five minutes to decide in Bayliss's favour. He received five thousand pounds, a huge sum at the time.

Only after this did the statue of the dog appear. Anna Louisa Woodward, founder of the World League Against Vivisection, raised money, and commissioned a bronze statue of the dog. The finished memorial stood over seven and half feet tall, and contained a drinking fountain for people, and a trough for dogs and horses. A home was found for it in Battersea at the Latchmere Recreation Ground, in September 1906. George Bernard Shaw was in the crowd at the unveiling.

The statue then became the focus for what we might later come to call student unrest. It was attacked in 1907 by a group of students, led by a sledgehammer-wielding undergraduate named William Howard Lister. Further attempts were made to vandalise and destroy the statue. At first a watchman was employed to protect it, and then there was a full-time policeman. And eventually there were the Brown Dog Riots. Given that only ten arrests were made, it's hard to see this as any great flowering of civil unrest, but it was enough to convince Battersea Council that this dog statue was more trouble than it was worth, and plans were drawn up to remove it.

In February 1910 there were demonstrations in Trafalgar Square and elsewhere, in favour of keeping the statue, but by then nobody seemed to want a riot any more. The statue was removed a month later and, by some accounts, given to a blacksmith to melt down. A new, less grand, statue was erected in Battersea Park in 1985.

One of the ten people arrested at the Brown Dog Riots was a Cambridge student named Alexander Bowley who, by all accounts, was arrested for 'barking like a dog'. If this sounds a little bit P. G. Wodehouse, it's worth bearing in mind that Wodehouse's last novel *Aunts Aren't Gentlemen*, published in 1974, has Jeeves caught up in a feminist demonstration in Trafalgar Square:

> Whatever these bimbos were protesting about, it was obviously something they were taking to heart rather. By the time I had got into their midst not a few of them had decided that animal cries were insufficient to meet the case and were saying it with bottles and brickbats, and the police who were present in considerable numbers seemed not to be liking it much. It must be rotten being a policeman on these occasions. Anyone who has got a bottle can throw it at you, but if

you throw it back, the yell of police brutality goes up and there are editorials in the papers next day.

But the mildest cop can stand only so much, and it seemed to me, for I am pretty shrewd in these matters, that in about another shake of a duck's tail hell's foundations would be starting to quiver. I hoped nobody would scratch my paint.

I think that's remarkably knowing, about both protestors and police, though I wish he hadn't used the phrase 'these bimbos'. Still, perhaps we can forgive many things in someone who's writing in his tenth decade, and who mocked Oswald Mosley so splendidly via his creation of Sir Roderick Spode and the Black Shorts. In *The Code of the Woosters*, 1938, Bertie says to Spode,

> The trouble with you, Spode, is that because you have succeeded in inducing a handful of halfwits to disfigure the London scene by going about in black shorts, you think you're someone.
>
> You hear them shouting 'Heil Spode!' and you imagine it is the Voice of the People. That is where you make your bloomer. What the Voice of the People is saying is: 'Look at that frightful ass Spode, swanking about in footer bags! Did you ever in your puff see such a perfect perisher!'

Riots do make good material for literature. Dickens's *Barnaby Rudge*, which was originally subtitled *A Tale of the Riots of 'Eighty*, seemed to understand the nature of riot pretty well, especially the intoxicating effect it can have:

> . . . sober workmen, going home from their day's labour, were seen to cast down their baskets of tools and become rioters in an instant; mere boys on errands did the like. In a word, a moral plague ran through the city. The noise, and hurry, and excitement, had for hundreds and hundreds an attraction they had no firmness to resist. The contagion spread like a dread fever: an infectious madness, as yet not near its height, seized on new victims every hour, and society began to tremble at their ravings.

In the early 1980s Linton Kwesi Johnson described a similar intoxication seizing the Brixton rioters in his poem 'Di Great Insohreckshan'.

> it woz event of af di year
> an I wish I ad been dere
> when wi run riot all owevah Brixton
> when wi mash-up plenty police van
> when wi mash-up di wicked wan plan
> when wi mash-up di Swamp Eighty Wan
> fi wha?
> fi mak di rulah dem andastan
> dat wi naw tek noh more a dem oppreshan

Some thirty years after the event, in a 2012 piece for the *Guardian*, he explained, 'I wrote those two poems (the other was "Mekin Histri") from the perspective of those who had taken part in the Brixton riots. The tone of the poem is celebratory because I wanted to capture the mood of exhilaration felt by black people at the time.'

Although, of course, that line 'an I wish I ad been dere' suggests it was written from the perspective of someone who *hadn't* taken part in the riots.

Maybe that's always the writer's best perspective, that of an observer rather than a participant, like Peter Hitchens. *Absolute Beginners,* Colin MacInnes's 1958 celebration of the liberating possibilities of class and sexual and racial difference, recounts how the nameless nineteen-year-old narrator witnesses, though doesn't participate in, the Notting Hill Riots, and realises that his pal Ed the Ted, the subject of much admiration and muted sexual longing, is on the side of the racists; at this revelation, the admiration evaporates.

As we read Monica Ali's 2003 novel *Brick Lane,* which for most of its length describes domestic life in the Bangladeshi community in Tower Hamlets, we know (even if we haven't read the book reviews) that a riot is on its way, a clash between Islam and anti-Islam, neither side having a very coherent idea of what they're going to be fighting about. Some local waiters, apparently with one voice, scream, '*You bloody bastards. What the hell you shitting on our doorsteps for? Go to Oxford Street! Go to hell!*' I don't think the waiters are deliberately echoing Shelley's 'Hell is a city much like London', but Monica Ali may be.

Still, the opaqueness of the event, and of its causes and motivations, the fact that the rioters don't quite know what they're complaining and rioting about, seems utterly convincing. The fact that in this case the riot turns out to be less dramatic than anticipated, in fact something of an anti-climax, only makes it more credible. Riots do not exist to provide neat denouements for works of fictions.

*

Maybe riots are always on Londoners' minds these days, in that they are either wishing to avoid them, or wishing to find one they can claim as their own. And so in the wake of the 2011 riots, which started in London but then (like many trends do) spread to the rest of the country, what could a poor *Daily Mirror* journalist do but interview Mick Jagger about them?

> I was kind of surprised that people were shocked it happened [Jagger said]. There's no warning, but it's a regular feature of English urban life if you think about it. Every ten years you get some riots . . . Riots like that have been a feature of Britain for two hundred years or so and we like to congratulate ourselves that it has gone away. But the reality is that they haven't, have they?

Some of us are still eagerly awaiting the Cheyne Walk riots.

EIGHT

Some Death, Some Disaster, Some Consolation

It takes a singular man to complain about the *quality* of murder, and for that we look to George Orwell (born in Bengal Province, famously down and out in London, lived at various times in Portobello Road, Maida Vale and Hampstead) in his 'Decline of the English Murder'.

In that short essay, written in 1946, Orwell laments, with some degree of irony, though in the end he means it, that murder isn't what it used to be. He reckons the golden age of English murder was roughly 1850–1925. Not all the murders took place in London, but a high percentage did, and most of the 'best' ones. This was the era of Dr Crippen and Jack the Ripper, good solid, London murderers, and Orwell names a number of others who are not so familiar to us today.

One of them, Neill Cream, is remembered, if he's remembered at all, as the Lambeth Poisoner. He was a Scottish-born doctor, who lived much of his life in Canada, and committed some of his murders in Ontario and Chicago, but having inherited money from his father he moved back to London, where he'd earlier done his post-graduate training. He settled in Lambeth, an area that was much in need of medical services but also well-supplied with prostitutes, his victims of choice. He poisoned at least five of them and was only caught because he tried to frame other, innocent, doctors for the crimes.

This was the kind of murder Orwell liked, committed by apparently good, solid members of the professional middle class, people with a lot to lose, and murders that involved what he called the 'finger of Providence', by which I think he meant that at some level they should be crimes of passion. And *that* Orwell, tells us, is how things were before the war, and these murders were a great pleasure to read about in the newspapers, especially on lazy Sunday afternoons.

Now, post-war, Orwell finds that 'the violence of external events has made murder seem unimportant', war has changed and ruined everything, and he settles on the Cleft Chin Murder as a prime example of the new kind of murder, which he finds only 'pitiful and sordid'.

The Cleft Chin Murder was committed by Karl Hulten, a Swedish-born American who joined the US army, trained as a paratrooper, and was sent to England in 1944 to take part in the D-Day landings. Once there, he deserted, taking an army truck with him, and headed to London, parking in Hammersmith, sleeping in the truck, and occasionally driving to military depots to refuel. He could hardly have gone unnoticed, but there was a war on, and he evidently raised no suspicions. He even found himself a girlfriend.

Hulten met Elizabeth Jones, an eighteen-year-old

Welsh girl who called herself a striptease dancer, though it seems she'd only ever stripped once. On their first date Hulten used his truck to knock a passing girl off her bike, and while she was on the ground he stole her handbag. Next day the pair gave a lift to a woman carrying two heavy suitcases. Hulten killed the woman with an iron bar and dumped her body in a river.

The day after that, Hulten and Jones hailed a hire car on Hammersmith Broadway and directed the driver to a deserted stretch of road, where they told him to stop. Hulten shot the driver in the back of the head, and later dumped the body in a ditch in Knowle Green, Staines, Middlesex. The murdered driver was George Edward Heath, and although the body was found soon enough by police, it took a while to identify him, except as a man with a cleft chin.

The day after the murder, Hulten and Jones, now in possession of Heath's car and money, went to the White City dog track. The day after that Jones decided she wanted a fur coat. Hulten sat in the stolen car outside the Berkeley Hotel and waited for a woman, any woman who happened to be wearing a coat Jones liked the look of, to emerge, with the intention of ripping it from her. In due course a woman in ermine became Hulten's victim, but she fought back, and before Hulten could take the coat, a policeman arrived. Hulten drove off but was arrested the next day in Fulham, where Heath's car was parked in plain sight.

The case was full of rich noirish detail, and the public lapped it up, but for the very reasons Orwell complained about. There was something big and desperate and irrational in the way that these crimes had been committed, so blatant and reckless, so extreme, so violent, so thinly motivated, some of the action taking place right in the middle of London. Hulten and Jones couldn't possibly have thought they were going to get away with it, and maybe they didn't want to. Certain sections of the public screamed for the pair to be hanged, and they got half of what they wanted.

Hulten and Jones were found guilty of murder and both sentenced to death. Hulten was executed at Pentonville Prison in 1945, but Jones was reprieved and remained in prison until her release in 1954.

Orwell was surely right in saying that 'the whole meaningless story, with its atmosphere of dance-halls, movie-palaces, cheap perfume, false names and stolen cars, belongs essentially to a war period'. However, another part of Orwell's complaint is that these murders were committed by 'an American and an English [*sic*] girl who had become partly Americanised', which sounds like fairly standard anti-Yank sentiment, of which there was no shortage in 1946 or has been at any time since.

But I think Orwell's most persuasive point is that when society is stable and well ordered, then a murder is something shocking and unexpected, a tear in the fabric of decency and order; it *means* something. When there's a war on, decency and order are destroyed, death and destruction become commonplace: murder becomes just business as usual.

*

Orwell was hardly the first or last person to have observed that people enjoy accounts of violence and death, of crime and punishment. Early in the eighteenth century *The Newgate Calendar* began publication. At first it was just a list of trials and executions, produced by the Keeper of Newgate Prison, but other publishers latched on to the idea and the name, attached subtitles such as the 'Malefactors' Bloody Register' and 'Villainy Displayed', and put out a variety of pamphlets, chapbooks and eventually encyclopedic collections, with the same title. These publications described the lives, deeds and inevitable, sorry fates of criminals. The works were popular and populist, ostensibly works of moral improvement in which readers could read and gloat over punishments while revelling in descriptions of the crimes.

The preface to a 1780 edition complains about other people's complaints, and runs:

> It has not been unusual, of late years, to complain of the sanguinary complexion of our laws; and if there were any reason to expect that the practice of felony would be lessened by the institution of any laws less sanguinary than those now in force, it would be a good argument for the enacting of such laws. [In other words, let's keep the blood flowing. And then] . . . we submit our labours to the candid revision of the public, nothing doubting that, on a careful perusal, they will be found to answer the purpose of guarding the minds of youth against the approaches of vice; and, in consequence, of advancing the happiness of the community.

You get the idea.

In various editions of *The Calendar* you can read about famous villains such as Dick Turpin, Moll Cutpurse and Captain Kidd, but there are plenty of stories about criminals who are otherwise lost to history. The Marquis de Paleott – 'An Italian Nobleman, executed at Tyburn for the Murder of his Servant, 17th of March, 1718'; Moll Raby – 'Who robbed many Houses, and was hanged at Tyburn on 3rd of November, 1703'; William Duell – 'Executed for Murder and came to Life again while being prepared for Dissection in Surgeons' Hall, 24th of November, 1740'; and many more besides.

There is also the occasional account of clemency, whether deserved or not, such as 'Francis Smith – Condemned to Death on 13th of January, 1804, for the Murder of the supposed Hammersmith Ghost, but pardoned soon afterwards'. The 'ghost' was actually an innocent plasterer named Thomas Millwood, who happened to be wearing white clothes when Smith spotted him and shot him dead. Still, the court decided that Smith had made a genuine (if utterly idiotic) mistake, and he was acquitted on the grounds that he thought he was acting in self-defence.

Charles Dickens certainly read *The Newgate Calendar*, just about everybody in London at the time did, and he has Oliver Twist reading a copy while he's in Fagin's lair: 'The terrible descriptions were so vivid and real, that the sallow pages seemed to turn red with gore, and the words upon them to be sounded in his ears as if they were whispered in hollow murmurs by the spirits of the dead.'

Dickens had higher literary ambitions than the writers and publishers of *The Calendar* but he wasn't above entertaining readers with accounts of strange and curious deaths. They appear throughout his magazine *Household Words*, published between 1850 and 1859. He and his staff wrote summaries of melancholy accidents, suicides and murders. Sometimes the tone seems to be railing against the cruelties of fate, but beneath that there's a cynical, knowing, tabloid-style indulgence in the sheer bizarre misery of the world, the two things not being mutually exclusive. The stories came from many places but the London ones seem especially telling, especially Dickensian.

In *Household Words* you can read about the two omnibus drivers committed for trial on the charge of Manslaughter by Furious Driving, having run over the keeper of a shellfish stall and his son in Great Portland Street. The son survived, the father did not.

There's Henry Harler who murdered his wife while she slept by cutting her throat, 'his mind unhinged by injuries which he imagined he had received from his wife's relations' – he was sentenced to death. There's Amelia Elizabeth Burt, tried for the murder of her child, whom she threw off Hungerford Bridge: she was declared to be of unsound mind and acquitted. There's Jane Collins a servant girl in the service of a cigar manufacturer in Mile End who killed her mistress's child and then herself.

Spectacularly, although I think it may lack the elements Orwell demanded, there's the double murder committed in Fitzrovia by a man named Bartlemy.

Accompanied by a young woman, he called upon a Mr Moore, a soda-water manufacturer living in Warren Street. After a while one of Moore's servants heard a voice cry, 'Murder,' then a gunshot, and by the time he arrived at the scene of the crime, his master was dead. Bartlemy ran to the front door to escape, but there he was confronted by a very brave neighbour, a Mr Collard. Bartlemy slammed the door in Collard's face, locked it and ran through the house into the back garden, so he could escape into New Road, a street that no longer exists. By the time Bartlemy got there, Collard had run around the house and caught him as he was jumping over the garden wall. They wrestled but Bartlemy shot Collard, fatally as it turned out. A passer-by, perhaps even braver than Collard, laid hands on the murderer and held him until police arrived. Collard was taken to hospital but he couldn't be saved. Even so he made a deposition that Bartlemy was the murderer and the latter was committed for trial. Bartlemy's female companion was never found. And I do wonder what the servant was doing in all this.

Are these London murders? Do they somehow epitomise the nature of the city? It's surely significant how often a London location or even a street address is attached to a murder. The Lambeth Poisoner we know; Jack the Ripper was originally known as the Whitechapel Murderer. The name John Christie is inevitably attached to 10 Rillington Place (long ago demolished). The Blind Beggar pub in Whitechapel Road is notorious because Ronnie Kray shot and killed George Cornell there.

It's hard to hear mention of Broadwater Farm without thinking of the murder of PC Keith Blakelock, and Blackfriars Bridge is inevitably associated with the death of Roberto Calvi 'God's Banker' who was found hanging there, hands tied behind his back, and bricks in his pockets. Who can hear reference to Cranley Gardens without thinking of the Muswell Hill Murderer, Dennis Nilsen – ex-policeman, civil servant, sex killer and cannibal, who picked up his victims in various gay pubs around London?

My own personal, trivial footnote to the Nilsen case: in a bit of morbid murder tourism that I wouldn't do these days, a male friend and I went for a drink in the Golden Lion in Soho, where Nilsen had picked up a couple of his victims. The place was quiet, and around the edges of the room there were single men, each sitting alone at his own small table. The guys were older, unhip, not very attractive, and no doubt they were harmless, still there was something that we found pretty creepy about them. They scrutinised us minutely. My friend said to me, 'If I went home with any of these men, being murdered would be the least of what I'd expect to happen to me.'

*

So, are you in any great danger of being murdered in London? The statistics suggest not. Murder rates fluctuate considerably year by year, and borough by borough, and since the numbers involved are comparatively small, it's difficult to make hard and fast judgements about patterns and trends, but there has been an overall reduction in the number of London murders since 1990. There were a hundred and eighty-four homicides in London in that year. In 2014 there were just eighty-three, though the number jumped to a hundred and eighteen in 2015. Overall the murder rate in London is currently about half that of Glasgow and about two thirds that of Belfast. Of course, statistics in themselves don't make us feel any safer, but they do surely suggest that we have less to complain about.

And assuming you're not murdered – a more than reasonable statistical assumption – you'll find that according to the Office of National Statistics, the death rate as a whole is surprisingly low in London, compared with the rest of the nation. Tower Hamlets has the lowest death rate in the entire country.

Naturally there are reasons for this. A lot of older people retire and move out of the city when they get the chance, even as more young people move in; just six per cent of the population of Tower Hamlets is over the age of sixty-five, but it's still something that Londoners as a whole may find consoling. In fact, according to a 2014 report by Professor Sir Michael Marmot of the Institute of Health Equity at University College London, in the most affluent areas of Westminster the life expectancy for women was 93.76 years, and 91.26 for men. Not that Marmot thought that was any reason to be complacent. In newspaper interviews he stressed that conditions varied widely across London, and said, 'The best life expectancy in London is better than the average in Japan, which has the highest in the world, and the worst compares to Guatemala.' OK, so yes, plenty to complain about there.

*

Comparatively safe as London may be, there's something about the city that invites disaster, and its size, its density, its complexity mean that disasters are always likely to be large scale.

Certain risks and dangers seem to be well behind us. We assume that London is relatively safe from plague, though that seems to have been a source of confusion even in its own time. Richard Baxter's *Autobiography*, published 1696, contains a section on the plague, in which he asks a lot of questions both about London and about God:

> Oh, how is London, the place which God hath honoured with his Gospel above all places of the earth, laid low in horrors, and wasted almost to desolation, by the wrath of God, whom England hath condemned; and a God-hating generation are consumed in their sins, and the righteous are also taken away, as from greater evil yet to come?

Some people are still trying to work that one out.

There's no reason to be complacent, yet a conflagration on the scale of the Great Fire of 1666 seems inconceivable. We don't fear that London will turn into a 'hell of confusion and torment' – that's Edward Waterhouse, in *A Short Narrative of the Late Dreadful Fire in London*, written in 1667.

Is London safe from flood? Well, the Thames Barrier, conceived after a great London flood of 1953 in which hundreds died, and finished thirty years later, was built to ensure that it is. Of course, situations change, and the Thames Barrier was constructed before there was much talk of climate change. The Environmental Agency intends to keep it operational until the 2070s, although some critics complain that it's no longer fit for purpose and that a new Barrier is required.

Dick Tappin who was one of the senior engineers and designers of the original project, and who continues to work on it today, has observed that the loudest complaints come from people with vested interests, the developers who think they'll get the contract to build a new one.

The earthquakes of London? Not much to complain about there you'd think, although London does feel the effects of an earthquake from time to time. There was a serious one in 1382 about which we have few details, another in 1551 and another in 1580, but these were small fry by earthquake standards, and the epicentre was a long way off in the Dover Straits. Just two people were killed in the 1580 quake, though Parliament was disrupted; also a trial of heretics, though for them that only delayed the inevitable.

A 1750 earthquake had London as its epicentre and Thomas Sherlock wrote *A Letter from the Lord Bishop of London to the Clergy and People of London and Westminster On Occasion of the Late Earthquakes.* He understood the earthquake as God's will, as he explained:

> It is every Man's Duty, and it is mine to call upon you, to give Attention to all the Warnings which God in his Mercy affords to sinful People: Such Warning we have had, by two great Shocks of an Earthquake; a Warning which seems to have been immediately and especially directed to these great Cities, and the Neighbourhood of them; where the Violence of the Earthquake was so sensible, tho' in distant Parts hardly felt, that it will be Blindness wilful and inexcusable not to apply to ourselves this strong Summons, from God, to Repentance.

Well, you can see how well that worked out.

The biggest UK earthquake on record occurred in 1931; it had its epicentre in the North Sea, some way off the coast of Yorkshire. Tremors were felt all the way down the East Coast, and even as far as London where, legend has it, Madame Tussaud's waxworks were shaken so violently that the head of Dr Crippen fell off.

Currently 'leading seismologists' say that London is overdue for another big earthquake, and complain that the powers that be aren't taking the possibility seriously enough, at least that's what they say when put on the spot by journalists, or when they're seeking additional funding.

*

Sometimes complaining actually does do some good, though it may depend on whose doing the complaining. The outcry over the Great Stink of 1858 certainly led to some desirable changes, an end to the dumping of untreated human and industrial waste directly into the Thames.

It was not a brand new problem. In 1855, Michael Faraday had written to *The Times* that, 'Near the bridges the feculence rolled up in clouds so dense that they were visible at the surface.' An 1858 editorial in the same paper dated 18 June said:

> What a pity it is that the thermometer fell ten degrees yesterday. Parliament was all but compelled to legislate upon the great London nuisance by the force of sheer stench. The intense heat had driven our legislators from those portions of their buildings which overlook the river. A few members, bent upon investigating the matter to its very depth, ventured into the library, but they were instantaneously driven to retreat, each man with a handkerchief to his nose. We are heartily glad of it.

Well, yes, that concentrated the minds of politicians wonderfully. By the beginning of August legislation had been passed allowing the Metropolitan Board of Works to borrow three million pounds to create a new sewage system, under the guidance of Sir Joseph Bazalgette, a system that's still largely in place today.

As for the London fog, or smog as it came to be called, complaints about that had been vented for a very long time. In the 1661 pamphlet *Fumifugium: or, The Inconveniencie of the Aer and Smoak of London dissipated together with some Remedies humbly proposed,* John Evelyn again took a somewhat spiritual view: a clean soul needed clean air; but he was practical too. He wrote:

> It is this horrid Smoake which obscures our Churches, and makes our Palaces look old, which fouls our Clothes, and corrupts the Waters, so as the very Rain, and refreshing Dews which fall in the several Seasons, precipitate this impure Vapour, which, with its black and tenacious quality, spots and contaminates whatsoever is exposed to it.

His proposed solution to the problem was to move industry out of the city and plant sweet-smelling hedges around the boundaries. The scheme wasn't taken up, and differing manifestations of the London fog continued for about three hundred years, getting to the point when a good thick London Particular could essentially close down the whole city. Things came to head with the Great Fog of 4 December 1952; yellow with sulphur and black with soot, it was claimed to have killed four to six thousand people (figures debatable as ever), and it finally convinced Parliament that something had to be done.

Harold Macmillan, then Minister for Housing, is on record as saying, 'We cannot do very much, but we can seem to be busy – and that is half the battle nowadays.' The Clean Air Act was introduced in 1956 but it remained a toothless bit of legislation until 1962, the year of the last great London fog, this one responsible for seven hundred and fifty deaths. Finally the government had to be seen to be doing something, to be taking complaints seriously. They introduced more stringent pollution controls for industry and expanded smokeless-fuel zones. It was not precisely what John Evelyn had recommended, but it wasn't so very far off.

Today London's air quality is a mixed bag. It seems to be better than that of many European capitals, partly because of the congestion charge which reduces the presence of private cars in the city centre, partly because of a cleaner bus-fleet, and not least because the city has started to spray the worst affected streets with 'pollution glue', actually a dust suppressant, a biodegradable saline solution containing calcium magnesium acetate, which is basically a 'green de-icer'.

This may be treating the symptom rather than finding a cure, but it's got to help, surely. On the other hand, according to researchers at King's College, the pollution levels on Oxford Street reached their annual limits for the entire year in the first four days of 2015.

*

Londoners clearly do have something to worry about when it comes to terrorism, worries that the citizens of, say, Jersey or the Orkneys just don't have. London's size, and no doubt its imperialist history, make it a target, while its size and the opportunities for anonymity make it easy for terrorists to remain undetected. Fears of the city becoming a Londinistan seem exaggerated yet not entirely unreasonable. The sub-post office in Formosa Street in Maida Vale, *my* post office, right around the corner from my flat, had a public fax machine that was used by Khalid al Fawwaz, accused of being leader of the London al-Qa'ida cell from 1994 until his arrest in

1998, though he denied this. Fawwaz was also said to be one of bin Laden's 'key lieutenants', and a man implicated in the bombing of the American Embassies in Nairobi and Dar-es-Salaam, though again he said otherwise. Fawwaz was sentenced to life imprisonment in the United States in 2015. The fax machine was not returned.

*

Events of 7/7, 2005, remain London's worst terrorist attack to date, with fifty-two killed and seven hundred injured. The fact that the attacks were against civilians using public transport suggested even before the terrorists were identified that the perpetrators must have had some knowledge of the city and of London Transport, though none of them proved to be Londoners. Three of the four attackers came from Leeds, one from Aylesbury.

Although Islamic terrorism has hardly led to nostalgia for the IRA, at least they gave warnings before they planted bombs and they used code words so police knew which were serious threats and which were hoaxes. Of course, Londoners complained long and hard about the IRA, but the actual disruption caused by suspect packages which led to the shutting down of streets and tube stations was more often thought of as a nuisance than as a threat to life.

I have an abiding memory of seeing many hundreds of commuters walking across Green Park after a suspect device was found at Victoria Station, leading to its temporary closure. I can't say those commuters were cheerful, and I'm sure there was a good deal of complaining going on, but nobody seemed remotely terrorised. They were stoic. This was just one more hassle that went along with living in London, just one more thing that had to be dealt with, one more thing to complain about.

After the 7/7 bombings an anonymous (and perhaps apocryphal) old Londoner was much quoted as saying, 'I've been blown up by a better class of bastard than this!' This same Londoner, or one very similar, or perhaps more than one, had said the same thing about the IRA bombings. The London Blitz remains the disaster by which all subsequent disasters are measured.

*

The 7/7 attacks occurred the day after it was announced that London would host the 2012 Olympics. In the run-up to the games there was a good deal of complaining about what the event would do to London. Fear of terrorist attacks was certainly on the list, but most complaints were more localised and quotidian. It was said the games were a waste of money, the so-called redevelopment was all a scam for property developers. In any case, nobody was interested, nobody cared about the Olympics, although at the same time there were complaints that there'd be an influx of spectators so great that it might bring London transport to a standstill. Ticket allocations were said to be chaotic and unfair, although if nobody was interested this surely wouldn't have been much of an issue.

Perhaps the most engagingly articulate complainer was

Iain Sinclair, the dark magus of Albion Square, in his book *Ghost Milk*, and elsewhere. He above all saw it as a grand and corrupt folly, 'economic adventurism' disguised as public works. Offered a 'flight' on the Emirates Air Line Cable Car, he found himself next to a German television reporter who demanded to know the whereabouts of 'the famous Pleasure Gardens'. Sinclair writes:

> I had to explain that, due to unforeseen circumstances – strategic road closures, denial of entry to anyone not possessing a ticket to events at ExCeL – the competition-winning, Boris-backed, festival-staging venue at the Royal Docks no sooner opened than collapsed, despite a £3 million 'loan' from Newham Council. This is remarkably swift even by the catastrophic standards established by millennial follies undertaken by New Labour.

The Boris referred to there is, of course, Boris Johnson, then Mayor of London. Sinclair's description of him 'clowning so effectively towards office, like an idiot emperor from Robert Graves' is hard to beat.

Johnson did have enough nous to address complaints about the Olympics head on. He wrote on article for the *Sun*, the newspaper read by all old-Etonian politicians. He wrote:

> Oh, come off it, everybody – enough whimpering. Cut out the whining. And as for you whingers, put a sock in it, fast. We are about to stage the greatest show on earth in the greatest city on earth, and if you believe

much of the media we are all in the grip of paralysing stage fright.

We've got an advanced case of Olympo-funk. We agonise about the traffic, when our transport systems are performing well and the world's athletes are arriving on time.

We worry about security, when we always planned to have a strong military role in making our games as safe as possible . . .

And so on. My natural inclination is always to believe the utterances of Iain Sinclair and to distrust those of Boris Johnson, and yet once the games were under way, my wholly unscientific survey of Londoners suggested that a kind of Olympic euphoria took over. They found far more to enjoy than to complain about.

And this surely is the nature of the London complaint, an exaggerated vision of just how dreadful things are, and how much more dreadful they're going to be in the future. But the truth is, things in London often don't turn out quite as badly as expected. The complaints arise out of fears that are never quite realised, out of a pessimism that isn't entirely justified. This, of course, is just another reason for complaint.

*

Finally, one way of dealing with the horrors of London is to imagine the city subject to even worse horrors, fantasy horrors, imagining you've *really* got something to complain about: that's pretty much the whole of J. G. Ballard's writing career, from the urban anarchy of *High-Rise*,

London on fire in *The Burning World* and London under water in *The Drowned World* to hurricanes and dust in *The Wind from Nowhere.* His novels take their place in a substantial pantheon of London dystopias.

If you're worried about too many aliens in the city, why not imagine it being invaded by Martians, as H. G. Wells did in *The War of the Worlds*? Or by the Daleks or the Cybermen from *Doctor Who*, or by evil plants as in *The Day of the Triffids.* If you think it's polluted, read *After London* by Richard Jefferies, which imagines London submerged beneath a poisonous swamp.

If you think London's overcrowded, why not imagine it depopulated the way it is in Danny Boyle's movie *28 Days Later* then repopulated by zombies? Worried about American tourists and being murdered on the streets? Then watch the movie *An American Werewolf in London.* If you think the government's bad, well at least it's not *1984,* with London reduced to being an outpost of the world government of Oceania. Nor is the current city in the grip of a fascist government that puts opponents in concentration camps, as in *V for Vendetta.*

You can sing along with the Clash's 'London Calling' – 'London is drowning, and I live by the river' – or with 'London's Burning' – 'London's burning with boredom now . . . London's burning dial 99999'. And, of course, you could possibly combine the two – if you're worried about London burning, then living by the river would seem to have its advantages, but there's no good reason to look on the bright side, obviously.

People have tried to imagine few actual London

Utopias. *In the Days of the Comet* by H. G. Wells has a comet land, which turns the city into a socialist paradise. In William Morris's *News from Nowhere* there's no need for a comet; the hero simply falls out of bed and wakes to find London transformed by a socialist revolution, although ultimately he misses the struggle. He doesn't find enough to complain about, which of course is the whole problem with utopias and Londoners. 'We can't get anyone amongst us to complain of his not always having his own way in the teeth of the community, when it is clear that everybody cannot have that indulgence. What is to be done?'

But let's face it, Utopian visions are really only for the planners, the architects, the politicians, the sages and mystics, not for those of us who live down in the grit and dirt and confusion and annoyances of the city. We complain about the solutions every bit as much as we complain about the problems. A future in which we'd have nothing to complain about, what Londoner would want that? The London complaint is not psychosomatic, though it may well be a state of mind. It's a condition for which there's no known cure. And nobody really wants one.

Some Last Words

While I was writing this book, I was well aware that an EU referendum was on the timetable, asking the all-too-simple question, 'Should the United Kingdom remain a member of the European Union or leave the European Union?' Remain or Leave: it didn't sound so complicated.

I can't say that the prospect troubled me much at the time, or that it seemed like anything to worry or complain about. At worst it was David Cameron trying to placate the Euro-sceptics in his own party; at best it seemed to be an opportunity for a broader debate about Europe and its discontents, and also its advantages. This seemed to be a debate worth having. Euro-scepticism was, and still is, by no means limited to the Conservatives, and the Leave campaigners, whether you agreed with any of their political positions or not, did seem to be addressing some genuine public concerns about sovereignty, economics and immigration, concerns that were not simply the province of little Englanders and racists.

Of course, we all expected that there'd be some ugliness along the way – though we never for a moment dreamed that an MP, Jo Cox, would be murdered by some maniac yelling, 'Britain first' – but it was still possible to believe that venting concerns or even (strictly metaphorical) blood-letting would be good for the body politic. But this is also to say that I assumed that when the dust settled, when the arguing was over, common sense would have prevailed. I assumed that the citizens of the United Kingdom would vote to remain in Europe. How could they not? Well, as we've seen, quite easily.

The fact that I, and so many people like me, got this matter so completely and utterly wrong suggests one thing above all else: that we educated, metropolitan, London-centric, *bien-pensant* Liberals didn't understand our own country, or at least not the parts of it outside London.

Yes, the vote was close, and many non-metropolitans around the nation voted to remain, but overall there were only three regions that had a majority of Remain voters, Scotland, Northern Ireland and London: 62 per cent, 55.8 per cent and 59.9 per cent respectively. This might affirm what so many of us have often felt and said, that London is not really part of England.

Less than a week before the vote, Neil Acherson (a Scottish old-Etonian) declared in the *New York Times*, on 16 June 2016, that 'bloated London' was the real problem.

> English nationalism, though inchoate, is spreading [he wrote]. For older generations, it was cloaked in British patriotism. But now, having watched the Scots and the Welsh win their own parliaments, England – with no less than 84 per cent of Britain's population – feels aggrieved and unrepresented.
>
> And so the English have gone in search of their own

identity politics, finding common cause with the general impatience with old political élites that is flaming up all over Europe. For now, their angry sense of powerlessness is aimed at the European Union. But the truth is that it's from bloated, privileged London, not Brussels, that the English need to take back control.

Lord knows how that would be achieved, but it wasn't hard to see his point. When a single city contains so much wealth, so much privilege, as well as the seat of government itself, there's a very understandable reason for focusing all your resentments and complaints on the capital. Meanwhile, within the capital, it was easy for disappointed voters to characterise the city as a beacon of hope and enlightenment in a land of provincial darkness.

Very shortly after the results were declared, an online petition was deployed, demanding a second referendum, inspired perhaps by the idea that Leave voters had to be forgiven because they knew not what they'd done, and should be given a chance to rectify their decision. Things went pear-shaped on that one pretty quickly when, first, it was discovered that the petition had been originally set up by a right-wing Brexit activist who had assumed it would be needed when Leave lost the vote. Then, after Remain had made the petition their own, the site was infiltrated by automated signing bots that added tens of thousands of fake electronic signatures.

One Londoner, James O'Malley, went a different way. With some degree of irony, though it's hard to tell how much, he set up a petition asking the new Mayor of

London, Sadiq Khan, to declare London independent from the UK and apply to join the EU as a city state. His wording:

> London is an international city, and we want to remain at the heart of Europe. Let's face it – the rest of the country disagrees. So rather than passive aggressively vote against each other at every election, let's make the divorce official and move in with our friends on the Continent. Mayor Sadiq, wouldn't you prefer to be President Sadiq? Make it happen!'

Mr O'Malley was no doubt a provocateur, but he did articulate a feeling that many Londoners have – arrogant and questionable to be sure – that they don't need the rest of the country.

*

As I write this afterword there's a feeling of waiting for the other shoe to drop. How it will land and whether it'll destroy anything as it falls, remains to be seen. Assuming that the UK obeys its own referendum and leaves the EU – a reasonable assumption but not absolutely guaranteed – we're told the process of detachment, the exit negotiations, will take at least two years. That's a long time in politics or anything else. However we feel about things now, we'll no doubt feel very differently by the end of the process, maybe better, maybe worse.

London will presumably change as a result, though at this point it's very hard to imagine in precisely what ways. Whether, and how, it will become less 'European' and more 'English' is anybody's guess, and it's a brave soul who tries to define what it means to be either European or English. However, the free movement of European citizens and Britain's participation in the single market are two of the major negotiating points. If both remain as they are then perhaps the texture of life in London won't change so much after all. Equally, given the current low value of the pound, maybe thousands of European tourists will rush into the city, making it feel even more 'European'.

As for the bigger picture, will the London bubble burst? Will international money leave London? Will corporate headquarters move out? Will all this make property prices drop? And even if they do, will they drop enough to be affordable to people earning ordinary salaries? I have no idea. Your guess may well be better than mine.

So OK, let's say that London *shall* be different as a result of Brexit. But London would have been different in any case, just different in a different way. Shall there still be things to complain about? New things? Different things? Things we haven't even thought about yet? Oh yes. Oh my, yes.